MATT AND TO[...]

ULTIMATE
FOOTBALL HEROES

NEUER

FROM THE PLAYGROUND
TO THE PITCH

DINO

Published by Dino Books
an imprint of John Blake Publishing
3 Bramber Court, 2 Bramber Road,
London W14 9PB, England

www.johnblakebooks.com

www.facebook.com/johnblakebooks
twitter.com/jblakebooks

First published in paperback in 2018
This edition published in 2018

ISBN: 978 1 78606 935 1

British Library Cataloguing-in-Publication Data:

A catalogue record for this book is available from the British Library.

Design by www.envydesign.co.uk

Printed and bound in Great Britain by Clays Ltd, St Ives plc

1 3 5 7 9 10 8 6 4 2

Papers used by John Blake Publishing are natural, recyclable products made from
wood grown in sustainable forests. The manufacturing processes conform to the
environmental regulations of the country of origin.

Every attempt has been made to contact the relevant copyright-holders, but some
were unobtainable. We would be grateful if the appropriate people could contact us.

John Blake Publishing is an imprint of Bonnier Publishing
www.bonnierpublishing.co.uk

For Noah and Nico,
Southampton's future strikeforce

ULTIMATE
FOOTBALL HEROES

Matt Oldfield is an accomplished writer and the editor-in-chief
of football review site *Of Pitch & Page*. Tom Oldfield is a freelance
sports writer and the author of biographies on Cristiano Ronaldo,
Arsène Wenger and Rafael Nadal.

Cover illustration by Dan Leydon.
To learn more about Dan visit danleydon.com
To purchase his artwork visit etsy.com/shop/footynews
Or just follow him on Twitter @danleydon

TABLE OF CONTENTS

ACKNOWLEDGEMENTS

First of all, I'd like to thank John Blake Publishing –
and particularly my editor James Hodgkinson – for
giving me the opportunity to work on these books
and for supporting me throughout. Writing stories for
the next generation of football fans is both an honour
and a pleasure.

I wouldn't be doing this if it wasn't for my brother
Tom. I owe him so much and I'm very grateful for
his belief in me as an author. I feel like Robin setting
out on a solo career after a great partnership with
Batman. I hope I do him (Tom, not Batman) justice
with these new books.

Next up, I want to thank my friends for keeping

me sane during long hours in front of the laptop. Pang, Will, Mills, Doug, John, Charlie – the laughs and the cups of coffee are always appreciated.

I've already thanked my brother but I'm also very grateful to the rest of my family, especially Melissa, Noah and of course Mum and Dad. To my parents, I owe my biggest passions: football and books. They're a real inspiration for everything I do.

Finally, I couldn't have done this without Iona's encouragement and understanding during long, work-filled weekends. Much love to you.

CHAPTER 1

WORLD CUP WINNER

Sunday, 13 July 2014

As Manuel sang the words of the German national anthem loud and proud, he tried not to look over at the famous gold trophy sitting a few metres away from him. It was so beautiful and so close. Manuel could have reached out and touched it when he walked out of the tunnel. But he didn't want to jinx it. The trophy didn't belong to them. Yet.

'Come on!' Manuel clapped as the music finished and the fans cheered.

The famous Maracanã stadium in Rio de Janeiro was packed and ready for the 2014 World Cup Final – Germany vs Argentina. Manuel's team had lost in the semi-finals of the 2010 World Cup and Euro 2012, but this time, Germany had made it all the way to the final. After thrashing the hosts Brazil 7-1, they were the favourites to win, but they couldn't underestimate a top team like Argentina.

'We can do this!' Manuel told the defenders in front of him.

Philipp Lahm, Mats Hummels, Jérôme Boateng and Benedikt Höwedes – they were more than just his teammates, for club and country. They were his friends. They believed in each other and worked together. That's why they were one game away from becoming Champions of the World.

Yes, Argentina had Lionel Messi, but Germany had Manuel. In Brazil, Manuel had consistently shown that he was the best goalkeeper in the world. It wasn't just his incredible reaction saves; it was his all-round game. Manuel was no ordinary keeper. He could catch, stop, tackle *and* pass. He was Germany's last line of defence and also their first line of attack. His teammates trusted him and relied on him.

'Jérôme, watch Messi when he drops deep!' Manuel called and pointed.

He never stopped moving, talking, organising. It all helped him to keep his concentration for the big moments, the moments when Germany would need their goalkeeper to save the day.

After thirty minutes, Argentina's Gonzalo Higuaín had the ball in the net. But Manuel already had his arm up, even while diving down. 'Offside!' he called out.

Manuel was right, of course. The linesman raised his flag. No goal – what a relief!

In the second half, Higuaín chased after a long ball. He used his speed to escape from the German defenders, but he couldn't escape from the German goalkeeper. Manuel to the rescue! He sprinted off his line to jump and punch the ball away from danger.

'Thanks, Manu!' Benedikt shouted, patting him on the back.

Manuel nodded modestly. He was just doing his job: being the sweeper keeper.

Argentina couldn't score past Manuel, but

Germany couldn't score past Sergio Romero either.
The longer the match went on, the more nerve-
wracking it became, for the fans and for the players.
Fortunately, Manuel was Mr Nervenstärke: 'Mr
Strong-Nerved'. Even though he was the last man,
he stayed calm and focused.

In the last ten minutes, Germany had several
chances to score.

'So close!' Manuel was groaning, putting his hands
on his head.

But he didn't switch off. He had to concentrate at
all times. A goalkeeper never knew when his team
would need him. In extra-time, Rodrigo Palacio
chested the ball down and ran into the penalty area.
Manuel was out in a flash, making it hard for the
striker to score. Palacio managed to chip the ball over
him, but it went wide of the goal.

'No more mistakes!' Manuel told his defenders.

He was already preparing himself for his favourite
battle – penalties. Goalkeeper vs striker, one on
one, the pressure, the drama – Manuel loved it. He
had been the shoot-out hero so many times before,

for Schalke and for Bayern Munich, but never for Germany. Would this be his moment?

No, because André Schürrle crossed to Mario Götze, who volleyed the ball into the net. What a goal – Germany 1 Argentina 0!

Most of the players and fans went wild, but not Manuel. He punched the air and then returned to his goal-line. There were still six minutes of football left to play before he could celebrate properly.

'Stay organised!' he screamed out.

Lucas Biglia flicked the ball into the path of Marcos Rojo. Danger! Manuel had one last bit of sweeper keeping to do. He rushed out, lifted the ball over Rojo's head and caught it on the other side. He made it look so easy.

Neuer! Neuer! Neuer!

It was the perfect way for Manuel to end a perfect tournament. At the final whistle, he ran and jumped onto the growing pile of his Germany teammates. He hugged every single one of them.

'We did it!' they cheered.

Back in 2009, Manuel had won the Under-21

European Championships with Mats, Jérôme, Benedikt, Sami Khedira and Mesut Özil. That night, they dreamt about the future. Now, that future had arrived. They had won the World Cup together.

Manuel put on a white Germany shirt over his green goalkeeper jersey. He wanted to wear the national colours and he was no different to the outfield players anyway. But soon he had to take it off because he had a special award to collect.

'…And the Golden Glove for Best Goalkeeper goes to… MANUEL NEUER!'

Manuel had kept out Cristiano Ronaldo's Portugal, Karim Benzema's France, Hulk's Brazil and finally Messi's Argentina. He was the number one sweeper keeper, the best in the world.

Manuel raised the trophy in one big hand and punched the air with the other. What a night! He was very proud of his own achievement, but he was prouder about his team's achievement. The World Cup was the trophy that Manuel really wanted to hold. It was his childhood dream come true.

'Yesssssssssssssssssssss!' he shouted, lifting it high above his head.

Fireworks shot up into the night sky. The party was just getting started.

The German League, the Champions League, and now the World Cup – the small skinny kid from Gelsenkirchen had won them all.

When Manuel was younger, lots of people had made the mistake of doubting him. Would he grow tall enough to be a goalkeeper? Could he make it at the top level? Was his style too risky? But he rose to every challenge with nerves and gloves of steel. He was a leader, a winner, and a goalkeeper extraordinaire. It was like he had been born with a football in his hands.

CHAPTER 2

A BALL IS A BOY'S BEST FRIEND

'Look, he loves it!' Peter said, reaching for his camera. He wanted to remember this moment forever – his son's smiling face when he opened his favourite gift.

For Manuel's second birthday, his parents had bought him his first football. It was only little, the perfect size for their son's little hands. As they helped him to unwrap the present, Manuel stared at the ball with wide eyes as if it was a big, sparkly jewel. Then he stretched his arms out towards it. He dropped it the first few times, but Manuel soon got the hang of holding it between his fingers. A big smile spread across his face and his family clapped and cheered.

'Well done, Manu!'

'Just you wait until he learns to throw it,' his mum, Marita, joked. 'We won't be laughing then!'

'Don't worry, it's a soft ball,' Peter reassured her. 'It can't do much damage!'

Marita wasn't worried about a few broken glasses. A happy family was all that mattered to her, and Manuel was certainly a happy boy right now.

'Can you look up at the camera?' Peter asked. 'Say "Cheese"!'

But it was no use; Manuel was only interested in his new football.

When their parents weren't looking, Marcel made the terrible mistake of grabbing the ball off his younger brother. Manuel wailed and wailed.

'What's wrong, Manu?' Marita asked, rushing over to her heartbroken son. 'Oh, I know what's wrong – you want your new ball! But where has it gone?'

Marcel had been caught red-handed. He stood there looking guilty, with the ball hidden behind his back. It didn't take their mum long to work out the truth.

'Sorry, I just wanted to look at it,' Marcel explained, giving the ball back to his brother. The crying stopped immediately, and the frown turned into a big smile.

'I know, son, but he's not ready to share it yet!'

Even a year later, Manuel still didn't like sharing his favourite football. It went everywhere with him – around the house, down the streets of Gelsenkirchen, on car journeys and on holidays. It was his best friend, even better than Marcel.

Every now and again, his mum washed the ball, but that wasn't easy.

'No!' Manuel said, shaking his head firmly. He refused to let go of it.

Marita had to wait until her son was asleep and then gently take it out of his hands. By the time Manuel woke up, the ball was clean and back in his bed.

At first, Manuel just carried the ball around, sometimes throwing it up in the air. But Marcel was determined to teach him a better use for it.

'That's it, kick!' he called out, making the

movement with his leg. He placed the ball right in front of Manuel's foot. All he had to do was copy his brother and swing his leg.

'No, kick!' Marcel repeated as his brother tried to pick it up.

After a little more coaching, Manuel understood the game and he loved it. As he watched the ball fly off his foot, he clapped and giggled.

'Yeah, that's it!' Marcel cheered. With a little more work, Manuel would soon be ready to play a proper football match against him.

Peter watched from the doorway and smiled. It was great to see his sons getting along so well. Peter wanted them to choose their own interests in life, but he had always hoped that they would choose football.

Police work was Peter's job, but football was his passion. When he lived in south-west Germany, he followed VfB Stuttgart. But before Manuel was born, Peter and Marita had moved to the north-west region. So now, he supported the local team, FC Schalke 04. He couldn't wait to take Manuel

and Marcel on a family day out to watch a match.
Who knew, perhaps one of them would even end up
playing for the club!

'Boys, shall we go outside and play in the garden?'
Peter asked. 'I'll even go in goal if you like!'

'Yes!' Marcel cheered.

Manuel loved to copy his big brother. 'Yes!' he
cheered too. For now, he would stay a striker.

CHAPTER 3

STRIKER TO KEEPER

As soon as the car stopped, Manuel flung the door
open and sprinted over to the football pitch.

'Be careful!' his dad called out through the
window. 'And good luck!'

What a disaster. Manuel was late for his first-ever
training session with Schalke's Under-5s team, the
'Mini-kickers'. The practice drills hadn't started yet,
but the kids were stood together in a group, listening
to the coach. It was very embarrassing to be late.

'Sorry!' Manuel panted as he joined the others.

The coach smiled. 'Welcome! What's your name?'

'Manuel.'

'Well Manuel, your timing is actually very useful. I

just asked if anyone was a goalkeeper, and no one put their hand up. What a surprise! When that happens, we have a rule here at Schalke: the last player to arrive at training is the first to go in goal.'

Manuel nodded. Even though he was the smallest boy there, he didn't argue with his new coach. He wanted to show that he was a real team player and besides, this might be a good way to get straight into the starting line-up. Maybe he would get to play as a striker another day.

'Good man!' the coach cheered, handing him a pair of goalie gloves that were far too big.

When Manuel played football with his brother, it was always on grass. At the local park or in their back garden, it didn't hurt when he fell over. If he dived to save a shot, he normally had a nice soft landing.

But this Schalke pitch was different. The surface was red ash, rather than grass. During the wet winter, it softened a bit, but this was summer. It hadn't rained in weeks. As Manuel threw himself down to tip the ball wide, he winced. The ground was rock hard.

'Great save! I think we've found our keeper!'

When he heard his coach's praise, Manuel stopped worrying about the bruises. If he got to be Schalke's Number One, he didn't care about a little pain. His body would get used to it.

'Right, I'm going to try to go the whole training session without letting in a single goal!' he decided.

Manuel was enjoying himself. Each shot was an exciting one-on-one battle, the goalkeeper vs the striker. Who would win? Each time the ball flew towards him, Manuel moved across, watching it carefully. He had to protect the goal from attack. He never took his eyes off the ball. If he lost concentration, he would make a mistake and lose the game.

In the end, a couple of shots did get past Manuel, but they were right in the corner and impossible to save. As he took off his gloves at the end of training, he was pleased with his performance.

'Are you sure you weren't a keeper before today?' the coach asked him.

Manuel shook his head.

'Well, you are now!'

In the space of an hour, Manuel had gone from striker to keeper. Soon, he had his own pair of goalie gloves that were the right size, and his own pair of trousers with extra padding all the way down the legs. Hopefully, his amazing saves would no longer hurt so much.

'There's no stopping me now!' Manuel told his brother joyfully. As he dived across the living room floor, he didn't feel a thing.

Manuel couldn't wait to make his debut for the Mini-kickers. He looked tiny standing there in the middle of the huge goal, but he was ready to be his team's superhero and save the day. He was Schalke's Number One, after all. He had the baggy yellow shirt to prove it.

'Well done, Manu!' his family clapped proudly on the touchline as he caught the ball and gave it a powerful kick downfield.

He was off to a good start. He rubbed his gloves together and waited to make his first important save. When his team was attacking at the other end of the

pitch, there wasn't much for him to do. He watched
the game; he had a drink from his water bottle; he
called out to the defenders in front of him.

'That's it,' his coach shouted to him. 'Keep
watching!'

Even as Schalke cruised to an easy victory, Manuel
stayed alert and ready to come to his team's rescue.
In the last few minutes, the striker dribbled into the
penalty area. This was the moment Manuel had been
waiting for – his first one-on-one! In a flash, he raced
out of his goal towards the ball.

When the striker looked up to shoot, he didn't
expect to see the goalkeeper right in front of him.
He panicked – what should he do now? Suddenly,
it looked impossible to score. He kicked it as hard as
he could, but Manuel spread his arms out wide and
blocked the shot. The ball trickled wide for a corner.

'Thanks, Manu!' his defenders cheered, giving him
high-fives.

After the final whistle and the team-talk, he
walked over to his family with a big smile on his
face.

'Bro, you were awesome!' Marcel said, giving him a hug.

'Well done, you were so brave out there,' his dad said. 'Like a lion, like a proper Schalke goalkeeper!'

'Did you enjoy it?' his mum asked, although she already knew the answer.

Manuel nodded eagerly. He wanted to play another match straight away. 'I loved it!'

As the Neuer family walked to the car together, the team coach came over to say goodbye. 'I've never seen goalkeeping like that from a four-year-old kid. It was incredible. Manu, you're a natural!'

CHAPTER 4

MANUEL & MARCEL

'Lothar Matthäus plays a brilliant through-ball and Jürgen Klinsmann chases on to it. He just has Oliver Kahn to beat…'

That was the beginning of a lot of childhood matches in the Neuer household. The player names often changed, but the storyline stayed the same – striker vs keeper, Marcel vs Manuel. Away from the pitch, they were best friends as well as brothers. But their football battles were always fierce and always competitive.

'I hope you're ready to lose today!'

'You must be joking! Those are big words for a little kid like you.'

'Don't worry, it's okay to lose to your younger brother if he's better than you!'

'Shut up! Why don't you put your hands where your mouth is?'

Manuel and Marcel had different rules for different places. When they played in the living room, the tennis ball had to be kept below knee height. Any shots higher than that might hit photo frames, vases, or even worse, windows. They didn't want to give their parents any reasons to ban their matches.

Slide tackles weren't allowed, unless both of their parents were out.

'I'm just popping next door for a minute,' their mum sometimes told them. 'I won't be long. You boys play nicely, okay?'

'Yes, Mum!' they said, trying to hide their excitement.

For that 'minute', the normal rules went out the window. Suddenly, the game was filled with pushes, shirt pulls and dirty slide tackles.

'Oww – you just kicked me in the face!'

'Sorry, but you know the rules – there are *no* rules until Mum gets back!'

Amazingly, Manuel and Marcel never broke a single photo frame, vase or window. That was mainly thanks to Manuel's brilliant reaction saves. If the tennis ball ever bounced up, he managed to catch it before it could do any damage.

'Phew, nice stop!' Marcel said, looking mightily relieved.

Their best matches, however, took place outside, where there was more space to play. In the garden, the football had to be kept below head height. Any shots higher than that might go over into the next-door neighbour's garden. They didn't want to waste time jumping over the fence and back every few minutes.

Out in the garden, slide tackles were allowed. In fact, slide tackles were the *only* tackles allowed. Wearing his trousers with extra padding, Manuel threw himself across the mud until there wasn't any grass left. There were only three things that could end their epic battles – hunger, darkness or their mum's anger.

'Stop, look what you've done to my lovely flowers!' Marita called out from the backdoor. 'And Manu, if you've torn another hole in those trousers, you'll be sewing it up yourself!'

During the holidays, Manuel and Marcel's one-on-one battles stopped. With school out for the summer, the local kids gathered at the park to play football all day long. Most days, there were enough of them for a proper match.

Marcel put an arm around his brother's shoulder and smiled. 'Okay, how about me and Manu against the rest of you?'

'No, not again!' the others complained. 'It's not fair. You two have to play on different teams.'

Manuel always started off in goal, but his football skills were too good for him to just stand between the posts. He soon made his way up the pitch, playing as more of a defender than a keeper.

'Who's in goal?'

'Manu.'

'So why is he dribbling forward with the ball?'

'We're playing rush goalie!'

It worked a treat. Manuel's team usually won, even when his elder brother was on the other side. Marcel didn't mind admitting that he was no longer the best footballer in the family.

The brothers spent their summers playing in the park until it was time for their trip to Ameland, a Dutch island just north of Germany. Manuel and Marcel looked forward to the holiday camp every year. Three weeks of fun, football and no parents – what was not to like about that?

The highlight of the camp was always the Island Cup, the big football competition. The winning team would receive a trophy and Manuel and Marcel were determined to lift it together.

'With you in goal, this is going to be our year!' Marcel told his brother confidently during the ferry crossing.

Manuel crossed his fingers and prepared for battle.

They didn't have the best team in the tournament, but that didn't matter because no one could score past Manuel. He saved shot after shot after shot, like a shot-stopping machine.

Then when their opponents got frustrated, Manuel's team scored on the counter-attack, thanks to his long throws and passes.

'What did I tell you?' Marcel said, patting his brother on the back. 'We're going to win this!'

Their team was through to the final of the Island Cup. With the rest of the camp watching, it was Manuel's chance to shine. As the match kicked off, he tightened the straps on his goalie gloves and focused.

Manuel didn't let his team down. He dived low to his right and low to his left. He jumped high to his right and high to his left. He was determined to keep a clean sheet, no matter what. He even saved a penalty. Manuel completed his perfect performance by setting up the winning goal.

'You did it!' Marcel shouted as he ran to hug his team's hero.

'No, *we* did it!' Manuel corrected him.

It was a very special moment as the brothers collected their first-ever trophy together. All of their football battles had been worth it. In the winning team photo, Marcel sat in the middle, proudly holding the match-ball. He was the captain, after all. Manuel sat to the side, still wearing his goalkeeper gloves.

For Marcel, that moment was the peak of his football career. For Manuel, it was just the start.

CHAPTER 5

JENS LEHMANN

Growing up, Manuel had three main goalkeeping
heroes. First, there was Oliver Kahn, Bayern Munich
and Germany's Number One. He was a big, strong
shot-stopper and an international legend. But in
terms of style, Manuel preferred the more exciting,
modern keepers.

He liked Edwin van der Sar, the Dutch keeper who
played for Ajax and then Juventus. Like Manuel, van
der Sar was comfortable on the ball as a last defender.
He didn't just stand on his line and wait for something
to do; he got involved in the game as a sweeper.

But Manuel's top football hero played much
closer to home than Holland or Italy. Jens Lehmann

was Schalke's first-choice goalkeeper and he had been for years. It was the only club that he had ever played for.

'I'm old enough to remember when he made his debut,' Manuel's dad Peter told him. 'He was a tall lad with a mop of curly hair and skinny legs like matchsticks. You could tell that he was talented, but he made a lot of mistakes in the early days. We didn't like him at first, but we came to love him in the end!'

Manuel couldn't ever imagine not liking Jens – he was awesome and so entertaining to watch. He made lots of great, athletic saves and he loved coming off his goal line to deal with danger. What would Schalke do without him?

Whenever the Neuers went to the Parkstadion to watch a game, Manuel made sure that they got there really early.

'I'm freezing and there's still another hour until kick-off!' Marcel complained. 'Dad, can I get a hot chocolate please?'

While his dad and brother tried to keep warm in their seats, Manuel went down to the side of the pitch for a closer view of Jens' warm-up. It wasn't like his youth football, where a striker just took shot after shot at him from different angles. Instead, Jens had lots of different parts to his routine.

He warmed up his hands by moving the ball through his legs and behind his back like a basketball player. Then he warmed up his legs with stretches and keepy-uppies. Finally, he warmed up his body by diving low and then jumping straight back up to catch the ball.

'I haven't seen that bit before!' Manuel said to himself. He was always eager to learn, especially from his idol. He often took a notebook and pen to write down any new exercises that he could copy.

Manuel also watched Jens carefully during the match. He was always doing something – jogging on the spot, or talking to himself, or organising his defence. Manuel did the same things to help him stay focused throughout the game.

Whenever Jens made a great save, Manuel cheered loudly.

Marcel looked at his brother as if he was an

embarrassing alien. 'It's not like we scored a goal,' he argued.

'Hey, that save was just as important as a goal!' Manuel argued back.

Even when he became a Schalke ballboy, Manuel still got to the stadium early. By arriving first, he always got to pick his favourite position – right behind the goal. From there, he got the best possible view of his hero in action.

'We love you, Jens!'

Goalkeepers hardly ever got the praise that they deserved. But every now and again, they got the glory. In 1997, eleven-year-old Manuel watched the away leg of the UEFA Cup Final on a big screen at the Parkstadion. Schalke had beaten Inter Milan 1-0 in their home leg, so it was all to play for.

'Come on, Schalke!' Manuel cheered, waving his blue and white scarf.

After ninety nail-biting minutes, the score at the San Siro was 1-0 to Inter. That meant 1-1 on aggregate – time for extra time. Back in Germany, Manuel kicked every goal kick and stopped every shot. It felt like he was the one in goal out there in Italy, saving the day for his beloved Schalke. After another half an hour of tense defending, the match went to penalties.

'Come on, Jens!' Manuel cheered.

Marcel couldn't bear to watch, but Manuel believed in his idol. A shoot-out was a goalkeeper's best chance to shine. Could Jens become Schalke's UEFA Cup hero? As Iván Zamorano placed the ball on the penalty spot, Jens rubbed his gloves together and took a deep breath out.

'Dive right!' Manuel whispered, his heart beating fast in his chest. It was a guessing game, but the most important thing was to pick a side and stick with it.

Jens dived to his left and made a brilliant save. Advantage Schalke! Manuel cheered but Jens didn't celebrate at all. He just got up and got ready to save the next one.

Jens guessed correctly against Youri Djorkaeff too, but he could only get his fingertips on the shot.

'So close!' Manuel groaned with his hands on his head.

It wasn't a disaster, however, because Schalke
scored all of their first three penalties. Jens walked
up to the spot, bounced the ball, and then handed it
to Inter's next taker, Aron Winter, with a smile and a
few words. He was playing mind games to put him
off. In the end, Jens didn't save Winter's kick, but he
didn't need to. It went wide.

Manuel punched the air as the Parkstadion
erupted with noise. The noise in the stadium grew
even louder when Marc Wilmots scored the winning
penalty. Manuel hugged his dad, Marcel, and
everyone else around him. What a night – Schalke
had won the UEFA Cup!

'I told you Jens was the best!' Manuel reminded
his brother happily.

Schalke's hero was at the centre of the wild team
celebrations. With one amazing save, he had led them
to victory. Watching the scenes up on the big screen,
Manuel felt even more determined to achieve his
dream of becoming a professional goalkeeper. And not
just that; he wanted to become a Schalke hero, just
like Jens.

CHAPTER 6

THE LAST MAN

'Hey, that wasn't your fault,' the Schalke Under-12s coach said, patting his devastated goalkeeper on the back. 'First, we gave the ball away in midfield and then our defenders went to sleep. So don't blame yourself!'

Manuel was sitting on his goal line, hugging his knees and staring down into the mud. Rain was falling down heavily on his head, but he hadn't moved since the final whistle. He kept replaying the goal in his head; the striker running into the penalty area, his heavy first touch, Manuel's slip as he rushed out, his fingertips brushing the ball as it flew just past him and into the net.

Manuel shook his head and wiped the tears from his face. 'No, it *was* my fault – I'm the last man. It's my job to stop them from scoring. I should have saved that!'

They had drawn the match, but it felt like a defeat to Manuel. There was nothing he hated more than conceding a late goal.

The Schalke coach sat down next to him in the mud. 'I used to be a goalkeeper too, you know. Sometimes, it feels like the worst job in the world, doesn't it?'

Manuel nodded.

'Do you want to know why I stopped? I didn't have the *nervenstärke.*'

'What does that mean?'

'It means a calm, tough mentality. That's what you're going to need if you want to be a top goalkeeper, Manu. When you're the last man, you're going to make mistakes. You're going to feel like things are your fault, but you can't worry about that. The best goalkeepers make errors and then forget about them and move on. Have you ever seen Jens make a mistake?'

Manuel nodded.

'And did he just sit down in his goal to dwell on that mistake?'

Manuel shook his head.

'No, he got back up and carried on!'

Manuel accepted the helping hand and got to his feet. His coach was right; it was no good feeling sorry for himself. He walked off the pitch and joined his waiting teammates.

'Are you okay, Manu?' the captain asked him.

He nodded glumly. 'Sorry about that one,' he muttered. 'I'll make it up to you guys, I promise.'

The captain laughed. 'Are you kidding? You've saved us a million times! I know you're amazing, but you can't save us *every* time. Don't worry, we'll win the next match. Just keep doing what you do!'

Manuel was learning important lessons about being a goalkeeper. There would be terrible moments, as well as great moments. He just had to stay alert and confident, no matter what.

In the next match, Manuel was back to his normal

self. He moved around his penalty area, organising his defence.

'Dani, don't get too tight to the winger. He's rapid!'

'That's it, Jan. You can beat him in the air!'

Manuel wasn't thinking about anything except that minute of that match. Schalke's last man watched and waited for any signs of danger.

Just before half-time, he was called into action. The striker won a header and flicked the ball on for the rapid winger to chase...

'Keep doing what you do,' Manuel told himself.

This time, he didn't slip in the mud as he rushed out of his goal. It was another one-on-one, his favourite battle. As the winger went to shoot, Manuel made himself look as big as possible. He wasn't the tallest keeper around, but he was brave, and he had long arms and legs to stretch out. It would have to be a very special finish to get past him. The ball crashed against his body and Dani cleared it to safety.

'Yes, Manu!' the Schalke coach cheered, giving him a big thumbs-up.

Manuel felt happy and relieved, but he didn't show it. It was no big deal – he was just doing his job as the last man.

With a few minutes to go, Schalke were winning 1-0. Manuel was determined to go home with a victory, and a clean sheet too.

'Stay focused!' he shouted to his teammates in front of him.

As the opposition searched for a chance to score, Manuel positioned himself in the centre of his goal. He could touch his crossbar and he knew where his posts were. He bounced on his toes, ready to fly through the air.

Eventually, the striker took a shot from the edge of the penalty area. Manuel dived across to stop it, but the ball struck a Schalke player on the arm. *Handball! Penalty!*

Straight away, Manuel thought about Jens in the 1997 UEFA Cup Final. That night, he had showed plenty of *nervenstärke* – and now it was Manuel's turn. He picked up the ball and rolled it between his hands. By slowing things down, he gave the striker more time for doubts. As he handed over the ball, Manuel looked into the striker's eyes and smiled. He could see the fear.

'Right, pick a side and stick with it,' he told himself.

Manuel waved his arms and bounced on his toes. He studied the striker's run-up and made a late decision. He guessed right. The penalty kick was heading for the bottom left corner, but Manuel got his glove down to tip it wide. It was a save that Jens would have been proud of.

'Yes, what a legend!' his teammates screamed as they ran over to hug their hero.

Manuel felt happy and relieved, but he didn't show it. It was no big deal – he was just doing his job as the last man.

CHAPTER 7

"SCHALKE SCHOOL"

Growing up, Manuel could see Gesamtschule
Berger Feld School from his house. He could see the
amazing sports facilities and the Schalke stadium
next door. At night, Manuel dreamed of studying
at Gesamtschule Berger Feld. Whenever he stayed
home from school, he sat watching the pupils out in
the playground. They looked like they were having
the time of their lives.

'Why can't that be me?' Manuel thought to
himself.

He liked his school, but it wasn't Gesamtschule
Berger Feld. Little did Manuel know that his dream
move was about to come true.

In 2000, Gesamtschule Berger Feld and Schalke had a great idea: 'We're neighbours, and yet we never work together! What if we combine football and education? What if we set up a "Schalke School"?'

To test their brilliant plan, Schalke needed a group of their best young talents. Manuel was one of the first players that they asked.

'Yes please!' he replied excitedly. It sounded perfect. He would be able to work really hard on developing his football skills without giving up on his education. He couldn't wait to get started.

'Schalke School' balanced study and sport brilliantly. When Manuel did extra morning training sessions at Schalke, he had catch-up lessons in the evening. His 'school' days now lasted from 7am until 9pm, but at least they were filled with football fun. There wasn't much spare time to hang out with his friends and go to parties, but Manuel didn't mind. He was totally focused on achieving his dream, no matter what.

'Don't worry, Mum, I'm not missing any of the "school" part!' he promised.

As long as he kept getting good grades, his parents

were happy. They just wanted their son to have a Plan B in life, just in case his great football career didn't work out.

'And the "Schalke" part is going well?' his dad asked. He was so excited about having a professional footballer in the family.

'Really well!' Manuel replied.

He was enjoying his new challenge at Gesamtschule Berger Feld. Suddenly, he wasn't the standout star, and that made him work even harder. There were lots of excellent footballers at the school: tough defenders like Tim Hoogland and Benedikt Höwedes, plus silky playmakers like Alexander Baumjohann and Mesut Özil. The competition helped to get the best out of everyone.

'I'm just glad there aren't any other keepers here!' Manuel laughed with his teammates.

'Not yet, Manu!' Tim teased, 'but I'm thinking about changing position. Standing in goal and watching the game – how hard can it be?'

'Hey, when have you ever seen me stay in goal?' Manuel fought back.

Whenever the coaches let him, Manuel liked to train with the outfield players. It was good for him to practise his ball skills because in matches, he used his feet almost as often as his hands. He controlled backpasses, started attacks with his long kicks, and tackled strikers.

'That's true,' Tim admitted. 'You're more like a sweeper keeper!'

Talent and team spirit took Gesamtschule Berger Feld all the way to the final of the 2001 German youth tournament. Their opponents were Poelchau from the capital city, Berlin. Their team included an athletic young player called Jérôme Boateng. Ahead of the big match, Manuel did his homework. He found out as much as he could about Jérôme and Poelchau's other star players. He was determined to win.

'This is your toughest test yet,' the Gesamtschule Berger Feld coach Arthur Preuss told them before kick-off. 'This is one elite sporting school against another. It won't be a walk in the park!'

In the end, they did win the final, but mainly thanks to Manuel's heroics. While some of his

teammates let their nerves get the better of them, he
stayed brave and strong. He didn't mind the pressure
of a big final. In fact, he enjoyed it. He had the
nervenstärke to save not one, not two, but THREE
penalties!

'Okay, I'm sorry,' Tim joked as the team celebrated
afterwards. 'I couldn't do your job – you're the best
goalkeeper in the world!'

Manuel was always happy to help, especially
when there was a trophy and a winner's medal up
for grabs. There wasn't a Man of the Match award,
but everyone agreed that if there had been, Manuel
would have won that too.

'Two out of three ain't bad!' he joked with his
teammates.

The Gesamtschule Berger Feld headmaster,
Georg Altenkamp, was delighted to have a shiny
new trophy to add to the school cabinet. Thanks to
Manuel and his friends, 'Schalke School' was off to a
very successful start.

CHAPTER 8

GROWING PROBLEMS

'What if I never grow tall enough to become a professional goalkeeper?' Manuel asked, kicking the grass around his goalmouth in frustration.

That was his biggest worry. Manuel was tired of shots flying over his head and just beyond his reach. He had done his homework. Oliver Kahn was six feet and two inches tall; Jens was six feet four, and Edwin van der Sar was nearly six feet six! Manuel was a long way behind all of them. That's why his local region, Westfalen, had dropped him from their team.

Manuel was serious but Schalke's goalkeeping coach Lothar Matuschak couldn't help but laugh.

'Kid, you're only thirteen! Just be patient and your growth spurt will come.'

Lothar hoped that he was right. He had been coaching young keepers for many years and Manuel certainly did not fit the usual physical type; he was still a small boy with a high voice. But Lothar saw something very special in Manuel – the boy was intelligent and brave, calm and confident. He was also so desperate to improve. Manuel worked twice as hard as the taller keepers. Many people thought that size was all that mattered in goal, but that wasn't true at all.

It wasn't just Manuel's attitude that Lothar liked. He also had awesome goalkeeping skills. Manuel's smaller height made him a lot more agile. With the ball heading straight for the top corner, Manuel could spring up into the air and tip it over the bar. Some of his saves looked impossible.

'How on earth did you stop that?' the Schalke goalkeeping coach asked.

Manuel's arms were also surprisingly long and strong. In one of Lothar's favourite training exercises, he placed three small goals on the halfway line. The keepers lined up in the penalty area and tried to throw as many balls as possible into the goals. Manuel won the competition every time and he kept getting better and better. He looked disappointed whenever he missed his target.

'Come on, give the other guys a chance, Manu!'

Lothar encouraged his goalkeepers to get involved in the team play. They were footballers too, after all! The Schalke coach loved Manuel's style. He could start attacks with his huge, accurate throws, and he could stop attacks as a sweeper. He read the game very well, especially for a youngster. Yes, he came out of his goal a lot, but he almost always timed it correctly. The risk was always worth taking if he could win the ball.

'Having Manu in goal is like playing with an extra defender,' Lothar tried to explain to the Schalke Academy Director. 'He's the future!'

But sadly, it wasn't just up to Lothar. The other youth coaches didn't share his positive opinion about Manuel. They wanted a traditional stopper who was big enough to fill the goal.

'Look at him – there's no way that he's a goalkeeper!' they argued.

Manuel knew that he was in danger of losing his place in the team. After years of hard work, was his time at Schalke about to come to an end? With everyone talking about him, it was hard to concentrate on his game. For the first time in his football career, Manuel lost confidence in his ability. Perhaps he wasn't good enough to become a professional, after all.

'I think I might stick with tennis instead,' Manuel told Marcel. He was a talented all-round sportsman, and he had other options.

His brother shook his head. 'You don't mean that. Don't lie to me – I'm your brother! I watch you play football every week and I know how much you love it. Just keep going!'

Marcel was speaking from experience. He hadn't given up on his love of football. No, he wasn't good enough to play, but he worked hard to become good enough to referee instead. Marcel was on his way to the Bundesliga.

'We're going to get there together,' he told Manuel. 'I've always wanted to give you a red card!'

Lothar could see that something was wrong. Manuel wasn't his usual happy, energetic self on the training ground. He looked distracted and he was making silly mistakes that he didn't normally make.

'Concentrate!' the goalkeeping coach shouted.

Manuel took off his gloves and threw them down angrily on the grass. 'I can't!' he shouted back.

Lothar gave him a minute to calm down and then sat down next to him. 'Look, kid, I know you're upset and worried, but giving up isn't the answer. Trust me, you've got what it takes to be Schalke's Number One. One day, you could even be Germany's Number One! I believe in you, but you've got to believe in yourself too. You've worked too hard to stop now.'

Lothar's pep talk helped but the real gamechanger was a trip to see the doctor. The paediatrician did some medical tests to work out how tall Manuel would become.

'Thanks, we'll have the results for you very soon.' Manuel had never felt so nervous as he waited.

He prepared himself for the worst by thinking about small goalkeepers. Fabien Barthez was only five feet eleven and he had won the 1998 World Cup with France! So was Iker Casillas, Real Madrid's new Number One. Height wasn't everything.

Lothar seemed to read his mind. 'One of my favourite keepers was a Mexican called Jorge Campos,' he said. 'He played at the 1994 World Cup and he was incredible! He wore these really colourful shirts with short sleeves like the outfield players. I've never seen a keeper leap like that! He was pure entertainment. Guess how tall he was?'

'Five feet eleven?'

Lothar shook his head.

'Five feet ten?'

'No, Campos was only five feet six. You're taller than that right now!'

When they returned to the doctor's office, Manuel took a deep breath. He would just have to deal with the results, whatever they were.

'Do you want to take a guess?' the doctor asked with a smile on his face.

This was no laughing matter! Manuel shook his head.

'Ok, so remember – this is only a prediction. We definitely don't get it right every time! Kids grow at different speeds...'

'Just give me the answer!' Manuel thought to himself impatiently.

'...So, the results! Our tests suggest that your full height will be at least six feet two, maybe even a little taller. By the look on your face, I think that's good news!'

Manuel was beaming brightly: six feet two – that was the same height as Oliver Kahn.

'There's no way that I'm giving up now!' he told Lothar. He was feeling more confident again already.

At the next Schalke meeting, Manuel's name came up again. 'We can't keep waiting for him to grow,' one of the coaches argued. 'We've got better young keepers, so let's just release him.'

'Don't do it,' Lothar replied firmly. He wasn't giving up on his star pupil. 'One day, Manuel will be the best in the world.'

CHAPTER 9

BACK ON TRACK

Manuel was very relieved to be staying at his beloved Schalke. He couldn't imagine playing anywhere else. This was his home.

'Don't you dare relax now!' Lothar told him. 'This is when the hard work starts.'

Manuel couldn't wait for the next step up. His tennis career was over; he was now fully focused on football. As he grew taller and taller, Manuel also developed in other ways. He became stronger and he improved his kicking and his decision-making.

'That's it! It's all about anticipation,' Lothar explained. 'You're the sweeper keeper, sniffing out the danger. Just remember, you're also the last man.

So, you can't get it wrong!'

It was fine for the doctor to get it wrong, however. Manuel didn't stop growing at six feet two. He carried on until he reached six feet four. 'I'm taller than Jens now!' he cheered. It was a very good height for a goalkeeper, and he was still as agile as ever.

Manuel was full of confidence and he quickly earned a promotion to the Schalke Under-19s squad. He was really pleased with his progress, but it felt like he was starting all over again. He was at the back of the line, behind older keepers who had lots more experience. But luckily, the coach didn't see it that way.

'It's simple – I'm looking for the most talented and dedicated player in every position,' Norbert Elgert told him. 'I know how good you can be, Manu. I've seen it many times! If you can prove yourself at this level, I promise you'll be my Number One.'

Challenge accepted! Manuel didn't mess around; he claimed that starting spot like it was a cross from a corner. And once he had it in his gloves, he didn't let go.

'I had a feeling that you'd prove me right!' Norbert said with a big smile.

Manuel was the talk of the club, and it wasn't just the youth coaches who were impressed. Just after Manuel's eighteenth birthday, the Schalke II manager Gerhard Kleppinger decided that he was ready for Northern League football.

'That's awesome news!' Marcel cheered down the phone. 'I'm coming to watch. Where is it?'

Playing at the Lohrheidestadion in Bochum wasn't the same as playing at the Parkstadion, but Manuel had to start somewhere. One thousand supporters on a Friday was his warm-up. One day, he would play in front of 55,000 Schalke fans on a Saturday. He was taking one step at a time.

Unfortunately, against Dynamo Dresden, Manuel didn't get the nice, comfortable debut that he was looking for. Within the first ten minutes, he was picking the ball out of his net. The goal wasn't his fault, but Manuel still took responsibility. He was Schalke II's last man now.

'Come on, focus!' Manuel shouted out to his teammates, but also to himself.

After that shaky start, things got better. Manuel

grew in confidence and Schalke II fought back for a 2-1 victory. In the last ten minutes, Dynamo Dresden attacked again and again but they couldn't beat the super keeper for a second time.

'We couldn't have won that without you!' Tim Hoogland said, giving his old schoolfriend a hug.

Manuel felt on top of the world as he walked off the pitch at the end. A few more performances like that, and he could be moving up to the Schalke first team.

'Jens has gone and Frank Rost won't be here forever,' Manuel told Marcel. 'The team needs a new keeper and the fans need a new local hero!'

With such clear ambition, Manuel was on his way to the top. After one game for the Germany Under-18s, he moved up to the Under-19s. In July 2005, he travelled to Northern Ireland to play for his country at the UEFA Under-19 Championships.

Manuel was looking forward to his first big inter-national adventure. The football world would be watching out for the 'next big thing'. That could be him!

Manuel wore the Number 12 shirt, but he played

every minute of every match as Germany's Number
One. Despite all his excitement, his tournament
began with disaster.

Fifty-five minutes into the match against Serbia
and Montenegro, Germany were cruising. They
were 2-0 up and Manuel had barely touched the
ball. But twenty awful minutes later, it was 2-2 and
Borko Veselinović was about to take a penalty to
make it 3-2.

Manuel couldn't let that happen. Calmly, he
sipped from his water bottle. He was in no rush. As
he jumped up and down on his goal line, Manuel
stared straight into Veselinović's eyes. 'You're not
going to score,' he muttered.

Manuel was correct. Diving low to his left, he kept
the shot out with his strong right hand. 'Come on!'
he screamed.

Sadly, even that wonder-save didn't help to wake
his teammates up. Germany lost their opening match
4-2.

'Let that be a lesson to you all,' coach Uli Stielike
shouted in the dressing room afterwards. He was

furious with his players. 'Even Manu can't save you when you play that badly!'

With their coach's words ringing in their ears, Germany bounced back with wins against Greece and Northern Ireland. They were through to a tough semi-final against France.

Manuel was up against another top young goalkeeper – Hugo Lloris. It was an entertaining battle, but after ninety exciting minutes, Hugo's France were the winners. Manuel's Germany were heading home.

'Well done out there,' Uli Stielike said, patting Manuel on the back. 'You didn't deserve to end up on the losing team today. Don't worry, you've got plenty of international tournaments ahead of you.'

Manuel hoped that his coach was right. There was a great new generation of German footballers coming through, and he wanted to be a part of it. Manuel didn't make the 2006 World Cup squad, but Bastian Schweinsteiger did, and so did Lukas Podolski, Philipp Lahm and Per Mertesacker. Those guys were only a couple of years older than him.

'I'll be joining them soon,' Manuel told himself.

CHAPTER 10

FIRST-TEAM DEBUT

There was no stopping Manuel. By the end of 2005, he was training with the Schalke first team. Some teenagers would have felt nervous, but Manuel just felt excited. Why not? It was an amazing opportunity to work closely with the club's main goalkeepers, Frank Rost and Christofer Heimeroth. Manuel tried to learn as much as he could from them, to continue his rise to the top. He even had a squad number now – 29.

'Don't buy a shirt with my name on yet,' Manuel joked with his brother. 'That won't be my number for long!'

Most Schalke training sessions ended with

a match. Rost went in goal for one team and Heimeroth went in goal for the other. Manuel was disappointed that he didn't get to show off his goalkeeping skills, but at least he got to show off his footballing skills instead. He was playing as an outfield player with top internationals like Christian Poulsen, Ebbe Sand, Hamit Altıntop and Kevin Kurányi.

'Manu! I'm free, pass!'

Manuel dribbled out of defence and played an accurate pass towards Kevin's feet. He was enjoying himself. For once, he was the sweeper but not the keeper. He was wearing gloves, but they were just to keep his hands warm. He let his feet do the talking instead, with lots of amazing tackles. Manuel's new teammates were very impressed with his performance.

'Have you ever thought about playing in defence instead? You'd be better than him,' Christian joked, pointing at the team captain, Marcelo Bordon. 'And a lot faster too!'

'Hey, I heard that!'

Manuel laughed along with the others. It was nice to feel part of the team's banter.

As the players headed back to the dressing room, there was a crowd of Schalke supporters waiting for autographs. It was usually only the big-name players that they wanted, so Manuel was ready to walk straight past and take a shower.

'What's your name?' a voice called out.

Manuel turned in surprise. Was the man talking to him? Yes, he was!

'Sorry, what's your name?' the man asked again, holding out a piece of paper to sign. 'You played well out there. Are you a new signing?'

Manuel wanted to laugh but he managed to keep a straight face.

'I'm Manuel Neuer,' he replied, 'your third-choice goalkeeper.'

For the 2005–06 season, it stayed that way. But as the 2006–07 season began, Manuel had moved up to second-choice, with only Frank Rost ahead of him. Instead of Number 29, he was now Number 12.

'I'd still wait one more season before you buy a

shirt with my name on it,' Manuel joked with his brother. 'Or I guess you could just get "1 NEUER" now!'

Frank was in goal for Schalke's first Bundesliga match against Eintracht Frankfurt, but he injured his leg in the last few minutes. Manuel's luck was in.

'You're starting against Aachen,' the manager Mirko Slomka told him.

Starting? In the Bundesliga?! Once the first wave of excitement faded, Manuel was filled with fear. What if he made a bad mistake in front of thousands of fans, including his own family? As the last man, there would be nowhere for him to hide. His first game could also be his last.

'How are you feeling?' the captain Marcelo asked him in the dressing room before kick-off. 'You look pretty calm for someone about to make their Bundesliga debut!'

Manuel was clearly hiding his nerves well. 'Yeah, I'm ready to get out there and play!' he replied, trying to look as confident as possible.

As Manuel walked out of the tunnel, the full roar

of the crowd hit him like a howling wind in the face. From that moment on, the adrenaline took over. This was the day that he had been working towards since he was four years old. His dream was about to come true. Manuel was about to make his Schalke debut!

The first twenty-five minutes went by without any drama. Manuel got a few touches of the ball and started to relax. But then their centre-back, Mladen Krstajić, got sent off. Schalke would have to play with ten men for nearly seventy minutes. That meant Manuel would have a lot more work to do.

'Stay organised! Keep your shape!' he shouted to his defenders. He wasn't afraid to make himself heard, even on his debut.

Schalke held on until the half-time whistle. Manuel breathed a sigh of relief. So far, so good.

'Keep up the good work,' Slomka told his team. 'Let's stay solid at the back, but also try to create a few chances in attack.'

It turned out to be the perfect plan. Schalke scored early in the second half and then defended brilliantly until the final whistle. Manuel didn't have to make any spectacular saves, but he didn't make any spectacular errors either. Despite his young face and blonde highlights, he played like he belonged in the Bundesliga.

'Schalke's new hero!' the other players cheered, giving Manuel high-fives and back slaps. He was really part of the team now.

'Good job, kid,' Slomka said with a smile. 'Nothing fazes you, does it? I reckon that was the start of a long and great career!'

A win and a clean sheet – a goalkeeper's dream debut. Manuel couldn't have asked for any more. He walked over to the Schalke supporters to thank them for their encouragement. He knew how much the club meant to them. He was a fan too, after all.

Still wearing his gloves, Manuel gave two big thumbs-up to the crowd. It was a day that he would never, ever forget.

CHAPTER 11

SCHALKE'S NUMBER ONE

In the end, Frank Rost's leg injury wasn't too serious. A few weeks later, he was ready to return to the Schalke starting line-up. What would happen now? Despite two clean sheets in two matches, Manuel moved back to the bench. It was frustrating after his amazing first taste of Bundesliga football, but he had to stay patient.

'My time is coming soon,' Manuel told himself. His surname said it all – 'The New One'.

For the months of September and October 2006, he watched and waited. It felt like forever. Manuel loved training with Frank and really respected him as a keeper, but he was desperate to play every match. He felt ready. The Schalke fans wanted him to play too.

'We need to give him a proper chance,' they argued. 'He's young and he's really good!'

After a 3-0 defeat to Stuttgart, the manager finally made the brave decision.

'Manu, you'll be starting the next game,' Slomka told him after training one day.

Manuel did feel bad for Frank but, at the same time he was delighted for himself. This time, he had been picked as Schalke's best goalkeeper. And their next game wasn't just any old game – it was against Bayern Munich!

'It's you against Kahn,' Marcel reminded him, thinking back to all their childhood battles. 'It's Germany's current keeper versus Germany's future keeper!'

As they walked out side by side at the Veltins-Arena, Manuel didn't look over at Kahn. He looked out across the pitch and he looked up into the packed and roaring stands. Manuel needed to look strong, even if his knees did feel a little weak.

Luckily, the adrenaline soon kicked in.

'You can do this!' Frank told him before kick-off. Despite losing his place, he still wanted to help Manuel. 'Just treat it like any other game.'

But it wasn't any other game; it was the biggest game of Manuel's young life. With the spotlight on, could he live up to his growing reputation?

Schalke got off to an excellent start. They were winning 2-0 as Bayern curled in the final free kick of the first half. Manuel just had to stay focused and deal with it.

'I can do this,' he told himself.

As the cross came in, Manuel rushed out of his goal to punch it away, but he bumped into his own defenders. The ball only went as far as Andreas Ottl on the edge of the penalty area. His shot was powerful, but it was straight at Manuel. Could he stop it? No, he couldn't move his legs quickly enough to make the block. *Nutmeg!*

Manuel pounded the grass with his fist. Why hadn't he just stayed on his line? That way, he could have saved it. He was so annoyed with himself. For once, he had made the wrong decision and now Bayern were back in the match.

'Don't worry about it,' Slomka said to him in the dressing room. 'Just go out there and save the day in the second half.'

Manuel did his best, but the match finished 2-2. As he left the pitch, he sighed and shook his head. 'What a complete disaster!' he muttered.

'No, it wasn't,' Frank replied, patting him on the back. 'You did lots of good things out there. Besides, you're a goalkeeper. Do what goalkeepers always do – learn and then move on!'

Manuel was sure that he had failed his big test, but Slomka kept faith in him. 'No, you're my Number One now,' he said.

With his manager's full support, Manuel didn't look back. By the time that Schalke took on Borussia Dortmund in the Ruhr derby in December, he was playing with lots of confidence. He belonged at the top level of German football.

Goooooooooooooooooooooooaaaaaaaaaaaaaalllllllllll llllllllllllllllll!!!!!!!!!!!!

1-0 to Schalke! Manuel threw his arms up in the air and turned to celebrate with the fans behind his goal. When they scored the third goal, the supporters were having a party, but Manuel kept his concentration. He wanted a clean sheet to go with the win.

Out of nowhere, Dortmund's Florian Kringe hit a vicious volley from thirty yards out. The ball travelled towards him through a sea of Schalke shirts, but Manuel watched it all the way. He didn't just stop the shot; he used his strong arms to push the ball far away from danger.

'Thanks, Manu!' Mladen Krstajić cheered.

At the final whistle, Manuel was a little disappointed, but only because he had eventually conceded a goal. But 3-1 was still a brilliant result in the derby, and it kept Schalke in first place alongside Werder Bremen.

'There's no reason why we can't win the league!' Manuel told his teammates.

He had only just become Schalke's Number One, but he was already thinking about trophies.

From February until May 2007, Schalke stayed top of the Bundesliga, but with just two games of the season to go, they were one point ahead of Stuttgart. Next up – Dortmund away in the second Ruhr derby.

'If we win this, the title will be ours!' Slomka told his players, although they didn't need any extra motivation.

It was a very exciting match with lots of chances for both teams. Right at the end of the first half, Dortmund took the lead and there was nothing that Manuel could do to stop it.

'Heads up, it's not over yet!' he told his teammates.

As Schalke attacked, looking for the equaliser, Dortmund found gaps in their defence. Alexander Frei's shot took a big deflection off Mladen's leg and flew towards the top corner. Manuel wasn't giving up. He flung himself across the goal to make an unbelievable save.

'Neuer! Neuer! Neuer!' the fans chanted.

But Manuel's work wasn't done. As the rebound fell to Kringe, he somehow got back to his feet in time to block the shot. Double save – Manuel to the rescue!

His teammates hugged him, but Manuel didn't care about being the hero. 'Don't thank me – just go up the other end and score a goal!'

They tried and tried, but they couldn't score. In the end, the match finished 2-0 to Dortmund. Manuel was devastated to lose the derby, but there was still one game left in the season. He still had hope.

'All we can do now is beat Arminia Bielefeld and pray that Stuttgart lose,' he told Mladen.

Schalke did win but unfortunately, so did Stuttgart. Manuel's title dream was over for the time being. It was a cruel blow to take but he was still only twenty-one. There was plenty of time left for winning trophies. After a few weeks of rest and sadness, he was able to look back happily on his breakthrough year.

'Manu, you've done so well,' his dad proudly reminded him. 'At the start of the season, you were on the bench and now you're Schalke's Number One!'

CHAPTER 12

STAYING STRONG

'Never be afraid to make mistakes,' Toni Tapalović told Manuel. The veteran goalkeeper was now one of Schalke's reserve keepers and he had lots of advice for the young Number One.

'I'm not!' Manuel replied defensively. He was Mr Nervenstärke, the fearless stopper.

'Good. You've got what it takes to be the best in the world, but you've got to stay strong.'

Manuel wasn't like most other keepers. He was brilliant with his hands *and* with his feet. He believed in helping his team, and not just staying on his goal-line. Manuel was Schalke's last man in defence and their first man in attack.

Manuel's strong arm was a very dangerous weapon, especially on the counter-attack. He could throw the ball over sixty yards down the field for quick strikers like Peter Løvenkrands or Kevin Kurányi to chase and score.

'Your throws are better than my kicks!' Tapalović joked on the training ground.

Over the years, Manuel had worked hard to find the right balance between accuracy and distance. There was no point in kicking the ball really far if it flew straight out of play. He was still improving his technique every week. Perfection took a lifetime of practice.

Manuel helped set up lots of goals, but his greatest assist came against Wolfsburg at the Veltins-Arena. His team were 2-1 down with 30 seconds to go. Schalke won a corner – one last chance to score. There was no way that Manuel was staying back. Although he rushed out of his penalty area all the time, he didn't get many chances to cross the halfway line. Manuel wanted to become a true attacking hero.

'Here!' he called out, moving towards the back post.

The cross landed near the front post, but Manuel didn't panic and rush back to his goal. Instead, he made a clever run towards the penalty spot, looking for a rebound. It was another risk worth taking for Manuel. The ball fell right in front of him and he struck it cleanly with his left foot towards goal. Kevin was there in the six-yard box to help the ball into the net.

Goooooooooooooooooooaaaaaaaaaaaaaaaaaaaalllllll llllllllllllll!!!!!!!!!!!!

'Thanks, but that was a shot, wasn't it?' Kevin teased as they celebrated together.

Manuel shrugged. 'Does it matter? We scored!'

There were lows as well as highs, however. Being a goalkeeper wasn't easy. Manuel was still young, and he was playing a lot of matches, in the Champions League as well as the Bundesliga. It was impossible not to make a mistake or two, and Manuel had a big reputation to live up to. The one time that he took his eye off the ball and let it slip through his hands, the German media laughed and called him 'Butter Fingers'.

'What did I tell you?' Toni reminded him afterwards. 'Stay strong!'

Manuel's problem was that his goalkeeping style was risky, sometimes even reckless. When his sweeping worked, it looked brilliant but, when it didn't, it looked really embarrassing.

In another match against Wolfsburg, striker Edin Džeko dribbled into the Schalke penalty area. It was 1-1 with five minutes left. Manuel was alert and ready to deal with the danger. He rushed out and slid in with his feet, but he totally mistimed his tackle. *Penalty!*

Manuel held his hands up to say that he was innocent, but the referee knew the truth. He gave him a yellow card, and Wolfsburg scored the spot-kick to win 2-1. Manuel's rash decision had cost Schalke the match.

'Stay strong,' Toni's voice kept telling him in his head.

In the next match, Bayer Leverkusen's right-back

spotted that Manuel was off his line, and lobbed the ball over his head. It was a spectacular goal, but many people felt that Schalke's goalkeeper was to blame.

'There's no need for him to be out of his goal there,' they argued. 'Neuer's problem is that he cares more about attacking than defending.'

It was tough to hear the harsh criticism but fortunately, Manuel was surrounded by people who believed in him and his style – his family, his teammates, Toni and Slomka.

'Manu, I don't want you to change,' his manager told him, 'Just keep learning and improving.'

Still, as Schalke travelled to Porto for the second leg of their Champions League tie, Manuel had a big point to prove. On an important European night, his team really needed him to stay strong.

Manuel didn't let them down. He made save after save after save. Crosses, headers, long-range strikes – nothing, and no one, could get past him. It was unbelievable.

Tarik Sektioui's header was flying into the net,

until Manuel somehow managed to stick out a strong arm to tip it wide.

'What a stop!' Bordon cheered.

In the second half, Sektioui had an even better chance. He looked certain to score but Manuel jumped up in front of him and blocked the shot with a flying leg.

'I've never seen anything like it!' the commentator shouted.

With TV cameras watching all over the world, Manuel was putting on a goalkeeping masterclass. Suddenly, his bold technique was the best thing ever.

When the match went to penalties, Manuel knew that Schalke were going to win. He was playing the best game of his life. There was no way that he could lose.

Manuel guessed wrong for the first spot-kick, but he guessed right second time. After diving low to punch out Bruno Alves' penalty, he gave a big thumbs-up to the fans. Thanks to his heroics, Schalke would soon be through to the Champions League quarter-finals.

Manuel's next save was even better. The shot was well placed, right in the corner, but he flew across his goal and pushed it wide with his right hand.

Jermaine Jones scored Schalke's winning penalty, but the victory was all about Manuel. The commentators called it a 'One-Man Show'. The players ran over to jump on their goalkeeping hero. The fans chanted his name over and over again.

Neuer! Neuer! Neuer!

Eventually, Manuel escaped from the middle of the team celebrations. He looked up into the swaying stand and smiled. The tough times had all been worth it. It was the best night of his life and he wanted to enjoy every last second of it.

As a goalkeeper, Manuel would play a lot of matches that he would rather forget. This, however, was one that he would remember forever.

CHAPTER 13

THE FUTURE'S GERMAN!

There were two reasons why Manuel couldn't wait for the 2008–09 season to end.

Firstly, Schalke were down in eighth position and that just wasn't good enough. Thanks to Manuel, they were conceding the fewest goals in the league, but they were having big problems at the other end of the pitch. Schalke needed to sign some new strikers and start again next year.

Secondly, the sooner the club season finished, the sooner Manuel would be off to the 2009 UEFA European Under-21 Championships. He had already made his senior debut for Germany, but this would be his first big international tournament. Manuel couldn't wait to show the world that he was his country's future Number One.

'Our Under-21s didn't even make it to the Euros in 2007,' he told his brother Marcel excitedly, 'so we've got some catching up to do!'

By 2009, Germany had lots of brilliant young players. Manuel was the only one left from the Under-19s squad that had lost to France in the semi-finals back in 2005. This time, he would be part of an awesome new team, including captain Sami Khedira, Mats Hummels, Jérôme Boateng and two of Manuel's old school friends – Mesut and Benedikt.

With so much talent and experience, everyone expected the team to do really well. This was one of the few trophies missing from Germany's cabinet.

'They're calling us a "golden generation",' Manuel said, reading out a newspaper report during the flight to Sweden. 'If we don't win this, it will be a disaster!'

'Well, we better make sure we win then!' Mesut replied with a confident smile.

That was not going to be an easy task, however. In

Group B, Germany would be up against England *and* Spain. Only two of the three European giants would qualify for the semi-finals.

Germany didn't score in their opening match against Spain, but at least Manuel made sure that their opponents didn't score either. Thanks to his strong saves, they picked up a valuable point.

'Well done, that's a decent start,' Sami encouraged his teammates. 'Now, if we win our next two games, we'll be through!'

In the end, Germany made it through with a win over Finland and a draw against England. Five points from three games was a little disappointing, but the team stayed positive.

'Look, we're still unbeaten and our best football is yet to come!' Manuel argued.

But when? Time was running out, and in the semi-finals they faced Italy, whose young attackers Mario Balotelli and Sebastian Giovinco were full of tricks and full of goals. Again and again, they got past the German defenders, but they never got past Manuel.

Giovinco with a curling shot. *Saved!*

Marco Motta with a powerful header. *Saved!*

Balotelli with a thumping free kick. *Saved!*

Manuel was putting on another goalkeeping masterclass. He was like a brick wall between the posts. Early in the second half, Germany scored a goal and that was enough for the victory.

'What would we do without you?!' Mesut shouted, jumping on the Man of the Match.

Manuel was proud to save the day for his country, but he needed his teammates to find their form quickly. 'Come on, we can play so much better than that!'

In the final in Malmö against England, everything clicked into place for Germany. At last, they passed the ball around confidently and got a bit of luck along the way. Gonzalo Castro scored the first, and Mesut scored the second with a wickedly swerving free kick. England just couldn't handle them.

'Stay focused!' Manuel called out to the defenders in front of him. They couldn't switch off yet. He wanted a clean sheet to go with his winner's medal.

On the counter-attack, Sandro Wagner cut in from

the left and curled the ball into the bottom corner.
Five minutes later, he scored again.

4-0 – the trophy was theirs! The whole Germany
squad ran over to celebrate with Sandro. The whole
squad except Manuel, that is. For once, he stayed
where a goalkeeper was meant to stay – in goal.
He raised his arms in the air and did a little dance
in his six-yard box. There would be time for proper
celebrations after the final whistle.

'We did it!' Manuel cheered at the end, with his
arms around Benedikt and Mesut. It felt incredible to
achieve their dream together.

With the pressure on, they had shown the talent,
desire and belief to go all the way. After the trophy
presentation, the German players got together for the
winning team photo. As the tallest player, Manuel
took his place in the middle of the back row. As the
cameraman clicked away, he jumped high above his
teammates, a big grin across his face. He felt on top
of the world.

The tournament was over, but it didn't feel like
the end for Germany's Under-21s. Instead, it felt like

the beginning of something very special. Manuel was returning to the senior national squad with the trophy and the Best Goalkeeper award. Mesut would join him, and Sami and Jérôme would surely be close behind. The 2010 World Cup might be a little too soon for them, but maybe in 2014…

'The future's ours!' Manuel cheered, with the medal swinging joyfully around his neck. 'The future's German!'

CHAPTER 14

BIG CLUB INTEREST

In the summer of 2008, Oliver Kahn decided
to retire, after fourteen amazing years at Bayern
Munich. It was sad to say goodbye to such a
club legend, but Bayern chairman Karl-Heinz
Rummenigge had to look ahead to the future for
successors of Kahn's calibre. Was Bayern's Number
Two, Michael Rensing, good enough to move up
to the Number One shirt? Or should Bayern look
elsewhere?

In the end, Rummenigge chose both options.
Rensing got the chance to prove himself during the
2008–09 season, and at the same time, Bayern also
scouted out other world-class options. As the top

club in the country, they preferred to sign German goalkeepers. So, who was going to become 'the next Oliver Kahn'? The top three candidates were René Adler at Bayer Leverkusen, Robert Enke at Hannover 96, and the favourite, Manuel Neuer at Schalke.

'He's young, he's brilliant, and he's only going to get better,' was how the scouts described Manuel to Rummenigge.

Rummenigge didn't need much persuading. Manuel was his first-choice signing, but would he ever leave Schalke to join Bayern? That was the big question because there was a fierce rivalry between the two clubs. In the summer of 2009, Rummenigge started the transfer talk.

'We want Manuel Neuer,' he told the media, 'and I believe that he is interested in coming to Bayern.'

But the new Schalke manager, Felix Magath, rejected that idea. 'I have Germany's best goalkeeper and he's not going anywhere,' he replied.

Rummenigge wasn't giving up that easily. It might take a while, but he was determined to sign Manuel. He had found the right man to become Bayern's new

Number One. After the Under-21 Championships in
Sweden, he tried again but the answer was the same
– Manuel wasn't for sale, and especially not
to Bayern.

'We'll keep trying,' Rummenigge said stubbornly.

Bayern weren't the only big club who needed
a new goalkeeper, however. Edwin van der Sar,
another of Manuel's childhood heroes, was coming
to the end of his amazing career at Manchester
United. Apparently, Manuel was at the top of Sir
Alex Ferguson's shopping list.

'Wow, Bayern Munich or Manchester United?'
Marcel asked his brother. 'That's a hard choice, but
it's a nice choice to have!'

Manuel tried to ignore all the big club interest and
focus on the new season ahead. He was determined
to help his hometown club to win their first
Bundesliga title since 1958. How amazing would
that be!

But without any top European football to play,
Manuel couldn't help thinking about his future.
Would he ever win the big trophies at Schalke?

When he watched the Champions League on TV, he felt jealous of all the goalkeepers. 'That should be me!' he thought to himself. Perhaps he would need to move on to reach that next level.

'Just see how you feel next summer,' Toni, his goalkeeping coach, told him. For now, Manuel was a proud Schalke player.

On Manuel's twenty-fourth birthday, in 2010, the team played away at Bayer Leverkusen. Manuel didn't have that much to do but what he did do, he did as brilliantly as ever. He dived low to punch away a long-range shot; he rushed out to close a striker down before he could shoot.

'We love you, Manu!' the fans cheered. 'Please don't ever leave us!'

When Schalke scored their first goal, Manuel pumped his fists. When they scored their second, he threw his arms up in delight, just like all the other supporters around him.

Another win and another clean sheet – there was no better way to celebrate his special day. After the final whistle, Manuel walked over to the fans with a megaphone and sang Schalke songs with them.

'We're going to win the title!' he cheered. He loved the club and he always would.

A week later, however, Manuel was no longer feeling so positive. Schalke walked into the Veltins-Arena as Bundesliga leaders, but they left in second place. With two goals in two minutes, Bayern Munich broke their hearts.

'Come on!' Manuel shouted, kicking his goalpost in frustration.

He was good, but he wasn't *that* good. He couldn't stop world-class players like Franck Ribéry and Thomas Müller on his own.

After getting so close to the league title, Schalke had let it slip away. It was the same disappointing story all over again.

'It's never going to change, is it?' Manuel muttered grumpily. It felt like his beloved club would always lose against the big boys of Europe.

The summer of 2010 started with more interest from Bayern Munich and Manchester United. But Magath's answer – for now – was still no.

'Manu, stay one more season,' the Schalke manager said. 'We'll be back in the Champions League and you'll be my captain. If after that you still want to leave, I promise I will let you.'

Should he stay, or should he go? It was the most important decision of Manuel's life and he needed to get it right. What if Schalke won the league as soon as he left? What if he didn't like living in Munich, or Manchester? What if the fans at his new club hated him?

Manuel didn't want to rush things. He was still young for a goalkeeper. Thankfully, there was a very good reason to ask for extra time. The 2010 World Cup was about to begin, and Manuel had just become Germany's Number One.

CHAPTER 15

WORLD CUP 2010

When he heard the terrible news in late 2009, Manuel was devastated. Robert Enke was a great friend and goalkeeper, someone that he really looked up to. But sadly, he had passed away.

'I just can't believe it,' Manuel said to René Adler, who was now their country's new Number One. The whole of Germany was in shock.

'I know, it's awful,' René replied solemnly. 'All we can do is try to win the World Cup for Robert.'

The 2010 tournament in South Africa was only six months away. Manuel was hoping to make the Germany squad, but he didn't expect to play much.

'It'll be a great experience just being there,' he

discussed with Mesut. 'It's our warm-up for 2014!'

That all changed, however, in April 2010, when René injured his rib against Stuttgart. He was back in action two weeks later, but he was far from 100 per cent fit. The pain was getting worse, not better. It was the most difficult decision of his life, but René had to do what was best for his country.

'I'm not going to the World Cup,' he told Manuel. 'The Number One shirt is yours now. Good luck, go and win it for Robert!'

Manuel's mind was a big mix of emotions – sadness for René, plus excitement, pride and fear for himself. What if he let the team down? Manuel was about to represent a whole nation of people in the biggest football competition in the world. Not only that, but he would be Germany's last man.

'Don't worry, you won't be doing this alone!' Mesut reassured him.

Manuel was glad to hear that Sami and Jérôme were also joining them in the World Cup squad. Together, they were the future of Germany and they weren't even the youngest members of the team.

New stars Toni Kroos and Thomas Müller were only twenty years old.

'Are your Mummy and Daddy coming to hold your hand?' Manuel joked with them.

The atmosphere in South Africa was incredible. Everywhere they went, they heard pounding drums and blaring vuvuzelas. It was a carnival of noise and colour: the blues of Italy and France; the greens of Algeria and Cameroon; the oranges of Ivory Coast and the Netherlands; the yellows of Brazil and Australia; the reds of Chile and Spain; and the blacks, reds and yellows of Germany.

Their tournament began against Australia, with over 60,000 fans watching. As the players lined up for the national anthems, Manuel took a deep breath and puffed out his chest. He was ready to make his country proud. Mr Nervenstärke, the amazing sweeper keeper.

In the end, however, Manuel didn't have much to do because Mesut, Thomas and Sami stole the show.

'4-0 – what a start!' Manuel cheered as he hugged his teammates. 'Next time, give me *something* to do!'

But with a surprise 1-0 defeat to Serbia, Germany came straight back down to earth. This time, Manuel did have work to do, but he couldn't block Milan Jovanović's close-range shot.

'Come on, he was unmarked there!' Manuel complained, pounding the grass with his fist. He needed more protection from his defenders.

To finish top of Group D, Germany needed to beat Ghana. At one end, Manuel won the match with his super saves. At the other end, Mesut won the match with a brilliant goal. 1-0 – the Gesamtschule Berger Feld students to the rescue!

Next up were Germany's big rivals, England. The 1966 World Cup, the 1970 World Cup, the 1990 World Cup, Euro 96 – there had been so many classic matches between the two nations. Manuel was feeling confident about this one.

'We thrashed them in the final of the Under-21 Euros,' Manuel reminded the others, 'so let's do it again!'

Manuel ran up and struck the goal kick powerfully. It flew high into the England half and bounced down perfectly into the path of Miroslav Klose. The German striker slid in to make it 1-0.

Goooooooooooaaaaaaaaalllllllllllllllllllllllll!!!!!!!!!!!!!!

While the attackers celebrated together, the defenders celebrated with the man who had set up the goal.

'What a pass!' Per Mertesacker shouted.

Manuel was pleased with his assist but fifteen minutes later, that joy was gone. As the ball entered the Germany penalty area, Manuel rushed out to punch the cross away, but he was too late to reach it. Matthew Upson headed the ball past his flailing arms and into the empty net.

Manuel was furious with himself. 'If you'd just stayed on your goal line, you would have saved that!'

He didn't learn his lesson straight away, though. When Frank Lampard took a shot, Manuel was off his line again. This time, though, the ball flew just over his head and bounced down off the crossbar. Phew – what a relief! Manuel got up quickly and caught the ball.

'The ball crossed the line,' Lampard argued. 'It's a goal!'

The referee shook his head and the match carried on. It was a very lucky escape for Germany, and Manuel in particular. This time, he learnt his lesson. He didn't change his style, but he made the right decisions. He made a great tackle on Jermain Defoe and then a great save to deny Steven Gerrard.

'That's more like it!' Manuel told himself.

At the final whistle, he fell to his knees and hugged Per and Arne Friedrich. Together, they had done it. With a 4-1 victory, Germany were through to the World Cup quarter-finals.

Manuel was looking forward to his battle against one of the best attacking teams around. Argentina had Ángel Di María, Carlos Tevez, Gonzalo Higuaín, Sergio Agüero and Lionel Messi.

'Bring it on!' he laughed with Jérôme, who was now the first-choice left-back.

When Thomas scored an early goal for Germany, Argentina went looking for revenge. Manuel was ready for them, though. Messi's free kick flew over his bar and he made comfortable saves from Di María and Higuaín.

'That's it, don't give them any space!' he told his defenders.

In the second half, Germany scored on the counter-attack. In no time, they were 4-0 up. Angela Merkel, the German Chancellor, was up on her feet in the Cape Town Stadium, clapping wildly.

'We have to go on and win this tournament now!' their coach Joachim Löw told them afterwards. Manuel was thinking about Robert, and he wasn't the only one. It would be a very special way to remember their friend and teammate.

Germany's next challengers were Spain. They didn't have one big superstar like Argentina's Messi; instead, they had Andrés Iniesta, Xavi *and* David Villa.

'Bring it on!' Manuel laughed with Jérôme again.

Spain had beaten Germany 1-0 in the final of Euro 2008. Manuel hadn't played in that match, but older players like Per, Miroslav, Philipp Lahm, Bastian Schweinsteiger and Lukas Podolski had, and they hadn't forgotten the defeat.

'It's time for revenge,' Philipp told his teammates.

Manuel didn't want his first World Cup to end,

especially not at the semi-final stage. As Pedro passed a lovely through-ball for Villa, he rushed out to make the save. Spain were playing brilliantly but Manuel wasn't letting anything get past him.

'Keep going!' he called to the defenders.

In the second-half, Xavi floated a corner into the box and Carles Puyol made a late run to meet it. The Spanish defender's header was so powerful that Manuel barely saw it as it came towards him. He stretched out his long left arm, but the ball flew past it and into the net.

'No!' Manuel shouted, throwing the ball in anger. After all his hard work, his team was losing.

The match ended 1-0 – Germany were out. Manuel felt numb. He had given his all but in the end, it wasn't quite enough. He ripped off his gloves. He wouldn't be needing them anymore.

'Hey, well played tonight,' Iker Casillas, Spain's goalkeeper, said as they shook hands near the halfway line. 'You've been unbelievable all tournament. Wow, you've got a very bright future ahead of you! Be proud and come back in 2014, better than ever!'

CHAPTER 16

ONE LAST YEAR/ FINISHING ON A HIGH

As Manuel dried his gloves on a towel in the goal, he looked up into the stands of the Allianz Arena. It really was an amazing sight and sound. One small corner was coloured blue for Schalke but everything else was Bayern Munich – the songs, the flags, the red power. It was so hard to beat them at their home, their fortress.

'Come on, boys!' Manuel shouted out to his teammates.

It was the spring of 2011. He was the Schalke captain now and this was the semi-final of the DFB-Pokal, the German Cup. Manuel was desperate to win a trophy for his hometown club. He was one step away from a final, but it felt like a giant leap.

'Let's get stuck in straight from the kick-off!'

Manuel's opponent in the Bayern goal was a young keeper called Thomas Kraft. He seemed a popular figure as he waved to the fans during the warm-up. What Manuel couldn't see were the signs saying 'Koan Neuer' – 'No to Neuer'. It didn't matter how good he was; the Bayern fans didn't want to sign a player from Schalke.

The Royal Blues started brilliantly. Benedikt's header was going wide but Raúl was there at the back post to get the ball back on target. 1-0!

As Kraft shook his head with anger, Manuel shook his fists with joy. He didn't get too excited, though. Schalke were winning, but Bayern wouldn't give up that easily.

'Right, I'm going to be busy from now on,' Manuel prepared himself.

He knew what he was up against. He had played against Bayern many times before and their team included three of his Germany teammates – Bastian Schweinsteiger, Thomas Müller and Philipp Lahm.

Manuel wasn't in the mood for letting in goals, especially against his friends. He was the safe pair of hands that Schalke needed, and Bayern Munich wished they had.

'Nearly there, boys!' Manuel cheered. The Schalke defence was standing strong.

At the final whistle, they celebrated like they had already won the cup. 1-0 at the Allianz Arena – nothing could beat a victory over their biggest rivals. Manuel and his teammates stood in front of their fans and clapped and cheered for ages.

'What a team performance!' Manuel shouted, hugging Benedikt. He was really going to miss days like this.

After years of talk, Manuel had finally decided to leave Schalke. He didn't yet know where he was going – Bayern? Manchester United? – but he was going somewhere else. After twenty years, it was time for a new challenge.

'We're really going to miss you, Manu,' Benedikt told him.

'I'm not going anywhere yet, mate. We've got

trophies to win!'

Not only were Schalke in the German Cup Final, but they were also in the Champions League semi-finals for the first time ever. After destroying Inter Milan, they now faced… Manchester United!

'Think of it like a job interview,' Marcel teased his brother. 'Only there are millions of people watching!'

'Thanks, what would I do without your helpful comments?!'

With Benedikt out injured, Manuel knew that he was in for a tough time in the home leg at the Veltins-Arena. In the third minute, Wayne Rooney cut in from the left wing and curled a shot at goal. After a big deflection, it looked like it was heading for the top corner. Even if it didn't reach the goal, Javier Hernández was there waiting for a simple tap-in.

It was all down to Manuel now. It took all of his height and athleticism to leap up and slap the ball away from the goal, and away from Hernández too.

That amazing piece of goalkeeping was the first of many. United attacked again and again but Manuel stopped shots from Hernández, Park Ji-sung and

Ryan Giggs. He felt unbeatable.

'Manuel Neuer is having the game of his life here!' screamed the commentators on TV.

After sixty-five minutes of saves, United finally got past him. Giggs and Rooney made it 2-0 but if it hadn't been for Manuel, it could have been 7, 8, maybe even 10-0.

'I can't do this on my own!' he screamed at his stunned defence.

At the final whistle, Manuel wasn't really in the mood for talking but his fan club was waiting to shake his hand.

'Wow, that was impressive,' United's keeper Edwin van der Sar said. 'You can have my Number One shirt right now if you like!'

'Congratulations, I think that's the best goalkeeping display that I've ever seen against us,' United's manager Sir Alex Ferguson said.

It was great to hear such praise from his heroes, but all Manuel could think about was Schalke's defeat. He was disappointed. No, he was more than disappointed – he was furious.

'We gave them way too much respect!' he told his teammates in the dressing room. They listened to their captain in gloomy silence. 'Where was our organisation? Where was our fighting spirit?'

Manuel was so desperate to finish on a high at Schalke. If they weren't going to win the Champions League, they'd have to win the German Cup in style.

In front of 75,000 fans in Berlin's Olympiastadion, Schalke thrashed Duisburg 5-0. With no saves to make, Manuel enjoyed watching his team's flowing football. He was itching to get out there and play as an outfield player.

'Can we swap?' he joked with Benedikt in the last few minutes.

The huge gold trophy felt heavy in Manuel's hands, but he still lifted it high above his head and waved it around. After five seasons at Schalke, he had finally won his first club trophy. As music and gold confetti filled the air, Manuel was having the time of his life.

'You guys organised a really good leaving party for me,' he joked. 'Thanks!'

CHAPTER 17

BEGINNER'S BAD LUCK

'It has been a very difficult decision,' Schalke General Manager Horst Heldt told the media in June 2011. 'In Manuel Neuer, we are losing an outstanding player and captain. But we have decided to accept Bayern Munich's offer.'

They didn't want to sell Manuel to another team in Germany, but it was the best offer on the table. £22 million was a lot of money for a club like Schalke.

It was a strange time for Manuel, as he said goodbye to his childhood club and made the big move to Munich. It was hard, knowing that the Schalke fans were so upset about his move. He felt sad, he felt nervous, but he also felt excited.

'I am really looking forward to this huge challenge,' Manuel told journalists, as he held up his new Bayern goalkeeper shirt for the cameras. There was no number on the back, but everyone knew what it would be – Number One.

Usually, a new club meant new teammates, but that wasn't entirely true for Manuel. He had already played many matches with Thomas, Bastian, Philipp, Toni Kroos and Mario Gómez for Germany. Plus, Manuel wasn't the only new Bayern signing from the national team.

'I thought you might need some help at the back!' Jérôme joked as they hugged.

With so many old friends around him, Manuel settled in quickly. There was a friendly atmosphere on the training ground – it was all about working hard and playing hard. He couldn't wait for the season to start, so that he could show the Bayern fans how good he could be.

'I just want them to like me!' he told his brother.

'They will,' Marcel reassured him. 'A few big saves and the Schalke thing will be forgotten!'

Bayern started the 2011–12 Bundesliga season against Borussia Mönchengladbach. Manuel made some good early saves to calm his nerves but after sixty minutes, disaster struck.

When the long ball bounced just outside the Bayern penalty area, it didn't look dangerous. Jérôme was there and he could see Manuel rushing out of his goal. 'He'll clear the ball,' he thought to himself. Jérôme left it to his keeper but the striker Igor de Camargo beat Manuel to the ball. His header looped over Manuel's arms, past Jérôme and into the net.

What a mix-up, what a terrible start! Manuel shouted at Jérôme, and Jérôme shouted at Manuel, but they were both to blame. In their first Bundesliga match at the Allianz Arena, they had lost the match for Bayern. The fans were not happy at all:

Booooooooooooooooooooooooooooooooooooooooooo ooooooooooooooooooooooooo...

'Stay strong!' Toni Tapalović reminded him. The goalkeeping coach had moved with Manuel from Schalke. 'That game's over, so it's on to the next.'

Manuel was a world-class goalkeeper. He was

old enough and experienced enough to know that
one mistake wasn't the end of the world. Once
everything had calmed down, he talked it through
with Jérôme.

'Let's put that behind us and get on with doing
what we do best. Friends?'

'Friends!'

With eight clean sheets in a row, the booing soon
stopped. By the start of 2012, Bayern were top of
the Bundesliga and still in the German Cup and the
Champions League. At first, Manuel just hoped for
one trophy, but as their winning run continued, his
teammates were talking about the Treble.

'We've won the Double loads of times,' Philipp
said, 'but no German club has ever won the Treble.
Let's be the first!'

Manuel loved the idea of going down in history,
but he knew that it was best to take things one
step at a time. He had learnt that painful lesson at
Schalke. Bayern had a lot of big games ahead of
them, starting in April 2012 with Real Madrid in the
Champions League semi-final.

'Cristiano Ronaldo, Kaká, Karim Benzema – we're going to have to be at our best to keep them quiet,' Manuel told his defenders.

'And don't forget about Sami and Mesut too!' Jérôme reminded him. They knew how deadly their Germany teammates could be.

Mesut played a great through-ball to Benzema. As he dribbled into the penalty area, Benzema went for goal. The powerful shot flew towards the top of the net, but Manuel used his strong right arm to tip it over the bar. The Bayern fans clapped and cheered for their super keeper.

'Stay focused,' Manuel told himself. That certainly wouldn't be Real's last shot on goal.

It was an exciting, end-to-end game, but Bayern won 2-1 with a goal in the very last minute. They had a one-goal lead to take to Spain.

'We can't just sit deep and defend for ninety minutes at the Bernabéu,' Manuel argued with his teammates. 'Real already have an away goal and they will score again – they always score at home! So, we need to score too.'

The second leg finished 2-1 to Real Madrid. After 180 minutes of football, it was 3-3. Thirty minutes of extra time later, the game was still tied. It was time for penalties.

Manuel was ready to be Bayern's hero. He had been practising for months. He didn't save Ronaldo's penalty during the match, but he was going to save Ronaldo's penalty in the shoot-out. He was determined.

Ronaldo went first for Real. Manuel jumped up and down on his line, trying to read his opponent's mind. Ronaldo went for the bottom left corner and Manuel got down brilliantly to stop it. *Saved!*

'Come on!' he shouted to the Bayern fans behind the goal.

Kaká went next for Real. He aimed for the bottom left corner, just like Ronaldo, and again Manuel stopped it. It was an even better save! As he got up, Manuel clenched his fists and screamed at the sky. He was so pumped up.

A few minutes later, Bastian scored to put Bayern through to the Champions League final. The whole team celebrated together next to the supporters.

'You're the hero, not me!' Bastian shouted as he gave his goalkeeper a massive hug.

Manuel was delighted with his big-game display. After an unpopular start at Bayern, he had become a fans' favourite. Now, he needed to go on and make them even happier by winning trophies.

Sadly, Manuel wouldn't be winning the 2011–12 Bundesliga title. Borussia Dortmund were running away with the league, but that still left two big finals to fight for.

The German Cup Final in May was meant to be Bayern's chance to get revenge on Dortmund, but it didn't work out that way. Bayern lost 5-2 and Manuel had a nightmare. He let Robert Lewandowski's first goal go straight through his legs, and he spilled the ball for the second.

'I should have saved that penalty too,' Manuel muttered to himself in the dressing room afterwards. Sometimes, being a goalkeeper was a horrible, horrible job.

At least Manuel had one last final to look forward

to, the greatest of them all. And Bayern had a special advantage over their opponents, Chelsea. The Champions League Final was taking place at the Allianz Arena, their home stadium.

'Come on, we can't finish the season without a single trophy!' Manuel told his teammates before kick-off.

He didn't look at the big, shiny trophy as he walked out onto the pitch. The last thing he needed was more bad luck.

It was a tense match, with very few chances at either end. When Thomas finally scored, it looked like Bayern would win. But from a corner, Didier Drogba scored an amazing equaliser. His header was so powerful that Manuel could only tip it up into the roof of the net.

'You can do better than that!' he told himself, as he angrily booted the ball away.

A penalty shoot-out was the perfect way for Manuel to make things right.

'We need you!' Bastian told him, staring straight into his eyes.

Manuel made a good save against Juan Mata, but Chelsea's other spot-kicks were unstoppable. For Bayern, Philipp and Mario scored, but who would go next? Toni? Arjen Robben? No, Manuel stepped up himself!

'I'm more than just a goalkeeper,' he told his teammates confidently.

He placed the ball carefully on the spot and took a long run-up. Nerves, what nerves? Manuel hit a perfect penalty into the bottom corner. Job done.

It all came down to Drogba. If he scored, Chelsea would win. Manuel dived one way, and the shot went the other. His heart sank as he looked over his shoulder and saw the ball cross the goal line. First the Bundesliga, then the German Cup. And now his Champions League dream was over too.

'Manu, there was nothing you could do,' Philipp kept telling him as he sat stunned in the goalmouth. 'We'll be back next year, I promise, and we'll win!'

CHAPTER 18

TROPHY TIME

Manuel's luck got worse before it got better. There were very high hopes for Germany as they travelled to Poland and Ukraine for Euro 2012. After doing so well at the 2010 World Cup, their team was now even stronger; Manuel, Mesut, Sami, Thomas and Jérôme all had two extra years of experience under their belts. There was lots of confidence in the squad.

'We can't face Spain until the final this time,' Per worked out. Their path to the trophy looked promising.

Germany started well, with three wins out of three in the 'Group of Death', against Portugal, the Netherlands and Denmark. After beating Greece 4-2, they were into the semi-finals. With Manuel leading the strong defence and the attack scoring lots of goals, the Germans became the favourites to win the whole tournament.

But after his disappointing club season with Bayern, Manuel wasn't getting his hopes up yet. Anything could happen in knockout football, especially against a top team like Italy.

'Watch out for Balotelli,' Manuel warned his defenders. He remembered the striker from the Under-21 European Championships. He was a real wildcard.

The Italians had a game plan and it worked perfectly. They defended well and then tried to catch Germany out with quick counter-attacks. Manuel loved to come out and play as a sweeper keeper, but he couldn't cover the whole pitch. And he couldn't make up for every mistake.

'Stay focused!' Manuel kept telling his defenders. 'Stay in position!'

But they didn't. Twice, Balotelli escaped and twice, Balotelli scored. Manuel sank to his knees.

What could he do? He was the goalkeeper and he relied on his defenders, just like his defenders relied on him. They were meant to be a team, but at the crucial moment, they had fallen apart.

'We learnt some important lessons today,' Löw told his devastated players. 'It's all about World Cup 2014 now!'

Manuel felt like he was cursed. His teams kept getting so close to winning things, but that wasn't good enough. He was determined to make 2012–13 a trophy-filled season.

'I don't care how we win,' Manuel told Philipp. 'I just want to win!'

That was why he had signed for Bayern, after all. To play for a big club who won big trophies.

The German Super Cup, in August 2012, was the first of the season, and it was against Dortmund. Manuel refused to lose another final, especially against their biggest rivals. When Bayern went 2-0 up, he did everything possible to protect the lead. Nothing was going to get past him. Nothing.

A trophy at last! Manuel celebrated with his

teammates, but it wasn't a big party. That would come later. This was just the start of a long and successful season.

Manuel had a brilliant team in front of him, but he was also on the best form of his life. The Bayern players trusted their star goalkeeper. He made more great saves than ever, from free kicks, headers, shots and one-on-ones. His reaction speed and decision-making were incredible.

'You're like a superhero!' Jérôme told Manuel as he rescued his team yet again.

It wasn't magic, though; it was a winning combination of talent and hard work. Every day, Manuel practised the same routines with Toni, over and over again. The routines were similar to the ones he had watched his hero, Jens Lehmann, do many years earlier before matches at Schalke.

Manuel dived to his left, then got straight back up to catch a second ball; he dived to his right, then got straight back up to catch another ball. Sometimes, they added extra parts and tests.

'How about here?' Toni asked, holding a ball in the

top right corner. Challenge accepted. From his knees,
Manuel had to spring up and touch it as quickly as
possible. It took a lot of energy, but it was all worth it
when he made awesome double saves in matches.

Manuel also worked on crosses. If he was going
to rush out into the crowded penalty area, he had to
get to the ball and he had to punch it far away. If he
missed or got the punch wrong, the attacker would
have an open goal.

'Always trust your instinct,' Toni taught him. 'You
know when to come out and when to stay on your
line. Once you decide, back yourself and be brave!'

By the following April, in 2013, Bayern had
secured the Bundesliga title. They only lost one
match all season and Manuel kept a record 21 clean
sheets in the 34 matches. This time, they celebrated
properly. At Schalke, Manuel had twice finished as a
runner-up in the German league but finally, he was a
champion.

After yet another victory at the Allianz Arena, the
club set up a stage in the middle of the pitch. With
70,000 fans cheering, it was trophy time. The Bayern

players walked out one by one, down the tunnel and along a carpet with the names of all the Bundesliga Champions. '2011 – Dortmund, 2012 – Dortmund, 2013 – Bayern Munich!'

The young players went first, then the first-team stars. Manuel was one of the last because he was one of Bayern's best. The gloves were off for his big moment.

'Manuel...' the announcer shouted.

'...NEUER!!' the fans shouted back.

He greeted lots of club legends on the way to the stage, including one of his goalkeeping heroes, Oliver Kahn.

'Well done!' Kahn cheered, shaking his hand.

Once he had the medal around his neck, Manuel got as close as possible to the trophy. As they waited for Philipp to lift it, the players bounced up and down and waved their arms around.

Hey! Hey! Super Bayern! Super Bayern!

Cannons of confetti shot up into the Munich sky. Red and white for Bayern, and gold for the Champions.

Hey! Hey! Super Bayern! Super Bayern!

Eventually, Manuel got his hands on the beautiful trophy. He raised it high over his head and screamed. It was the best feeling ever.

After that, the fun started. The players ran around the pitch pouring big glasses of German beer over each other and even over their manager, Jupp Heynckes.

For one night only, the Bayern players relaxed and enjoyed the party. But after that, it was back to the training ground. They had the Treble to win.

CHAPTER 19

THE TREBLE

Saturday, 25 May 2013

The familiar football anthem rang out around a packed Wembley stadium. It was time for Bayern Munich vs Borussia Dortmund in the Champions League Final.

Just like Philipp had promised, Bayern were back and this time, it would be different. Still, Manuel didn't look at the trophy as he walked out onto the pitch. They didn't need any more bad luck after the 2012 final against Chelsea in Munich. Manuel hadn't forgotten that night, and neither had his teammates. They couldn't let that happen again.

Manuel was a man on a shot-stopping mission. He kept two clean sheets against Juventus in the quarter-finals and then two clean sheets against Barcelona in the semi-finals. No-one could score past him.

'Come on lads!' Manuel shouted. 'We beat these guys to the Bundesliga title and now we're going to beat them to the Champions League trophy too.'

Robert Lewandowski was one of the best finishers he had ever played against. At Schalke and now at Bayern, Manuel always looked forward to his battles against Dortmund's star striker. Who would be victorious at Wembley?

Lewandowski got the ball and turned into space. He was thirty yards from goal, but he could score from anywhere. His shot dipped and swerved, but Manuel was prepared. *Saved!*

For his next trick, Manuel did the splits to block Jakub Błaszczykowski's shot with his leg.

'Are you okay?' Jérôme asked, offering a hand to help his keeper up. It looked painful.

'I'm fine!' Manuel replied. Thanks to all his training with Toni, he was a good gymnast.

When Lewandowski ran into the penalty area, Manuel didn't rush out as he often did. Instead, he stood tall and waited for the right moment to block the shot. *Saved!*

At half-time, it was still 0-0, but only thanks to Manuel. He was keeping his team in the match.

'We just need to calm down and play our way,' Heynckes told his players. 'There's no rush!'

In the second half, Bayern took the lead, but it didn't last long. Bayern's Brazilian defender, Dante, fouled Marco Reus in the box. Penalty! Manuel did his best to put off Ilkay Gündogan, but he dived the wrong way. 1-1.

Bayern dominated the last half-hour of the game. From his goal, Manuel watched nervously as his teammates missed chance after chance. Would there be another penalty shoot-out in the Champions League final?

But out of nowhere, Arjen Robben dribbled through and scored. 2-1 to Bayern! Manuel pumped his fists and then focused. Just five more minutes. There would be no late equaliser this time. Manuel would make sure of that.

At the final whistle, Dante jumped into Manuel's

arms. It was a magical moment to share with his friend and teammate.

'We did it!' they cheered together.

The Bayern players had bounced back brilliantly from the heartache of 2012 to win it in 2013. Manuel was so proud of the team's achievement. They deserved it for all their hard work and resilience.

After celebrating down on the pitch, Manuel made his way up the stadium steps to the balcony to collect his winner's medal and, most important of all, the Champions League trophy. He gave high-fives to all the ecstatic Bayern supporters that he passed.

'Manu, you saved us tonight!'

Arjen was the official Man of the Match, but Manuel won the fans' award. Marcel had been right; his Schalke past had been forgotten and forgiven. He had become a Bayern hero.

Manuel was getting used to winning things now. He chatted happily with German Chancellor Angela Merkel and UEFA President Michel Platini. He waved to his family down below. It was great to have them with him for his proudest moment yet.

Other players kissed or touched the trophy, but Manuel walked straight past it. He was happy to wait for his turn. A few more minutes didn't matter. Finally, he held it in his big hands.

'Don't drop it!' Thomas joked.

Manuel laughed. 'When have I ever dropped anything?'

He passed it to Thomas and lifted him up on his shoulders. They were the Champions of Europe! It didn't get any better than that.

After that wild night at Wembley, it was back to training. Bayern's amazing season still wasn't over.

'Two down, one to go,' Heynckes reminded the players. 'No German team has ever won the Treble!'

In the German Cup Final, they faced Stuttgart. Manuel was pleased that it wasn't Lewandowski's Dortmund again, but that didn't mean they could take it easy. It was a cup final – anything could happen.

'Let's keep our eyes on the prize today!' he told the defenders.

When Bayern raced into a 3-0 lead, some of the players started thinking about their holidays. That was a mistake, though, because Stuttgart fought back. Manuel made a double save but he couldn't make a triple save. 3-2!

'Come on, I need some help here!' he screamed at his teammates. 'We're throwing this away!'

It was an anxious last 15 minutes, but Bayern held on to win the Treble. Although Manuel wasn't pleased with the second-half performance, the result was all that mattered. He walked around the pitch with a big smile on his face and three fingers up in the air. They had done it.

'We just made history!' Bastian shouted over the noise of the fans.

Hey! Hey! Super Bayern! Super Bayern!

'What a season!' Manuel replied.

He was delighted but also a little relieved. This time, there were no more matches to play. Manuel and his teammates could take a well-earned break and enjoy their once-in-a-lifetime achievement.

Or was it?

'Same time, next year?' he asked.

Bastian laughed but Manuel wasn't joking.

CHAPTER 20

PEP TALK

Manuel's breaks never lasted long. Soon, he was eager to get back to football. He couldn't wait for preseason training to start. Things were changing at Bayern. He had top new teammates like Mario Götze and Thiago Alcântara, and a top new manager too – Pep Guardiola.

'The guy's a genius,' Manuel argued. 'Look at what he did at Barcelona – he's going to make us even better!'

That was going to be a very difficult job because Bayern had just won the Treble. They were already the Champions of Europe. What else was there left to win? It wasn't just about winning, though; it was also about style. Pep's Barcelona team won everything *and* played beautiful, passing football.

For Manuel, the most exciting part was Pep's modern goalkeeping plans. Guardiola liked his Number One to play like an eleventh outfield player. At Barcelona, he taught Víctor Valdés to play the sweeper keeper role. He became the last line of defence and the first line of attack. At Bayern, Manuel wouldn't need to be taught to play like that. He was already that kind of keeper.

He impressed his new manager right from the start. In the UEFA Super Cup, Bayern faced Chelsea, the team that had beaten them in the 2012 Champions League Final. Manuel wanted revenge, especially when the match went to penalties again.

'You can do this!' Toni told him, going through their notes on Chelsea's penalty-takers.

Manuel didn't save any of the first four Chelsea spot-kicks, but he didn't give up. With one strong stop, he won another trophy for Bayern.

'What a hero!' Philipp cheered as the whole team ran to celebrate with their goalkeeper. How many times had he saved the day?

Pep loved Manuel's style and encouraged him to get even more involved. 'Just because you're allowed to use your hands, doesn't mean you shouldn't use your feet. You're a good footballer – I've seen it! Don't be afraid to come out and play. That's what I want you to do!'

In training, Pep often took Manuel away from his goalkeeper routines to work with the defenders instead. Now that the Bayern team was pushing higher up the pitch, Manuel was the king of more than just his penalty area. He was the king of his whole half! He loved the freedom and responsibility of his new role.

In one game, Manuel received a short back-pass from Jérôme. Did he panic? No, he calmly chipped it just over the striker's head and back to his defender.

Olé!

In another game, Manuel rushed out of his goal and cleared the ball with a diving header. A few minutes later, he headed the ball over a striker and ran on to his own pass.

Olé!

Cruyff turns, cheeky flicks – Manuel wasn't afraid to try anything. In one game, he even took a throw-in!

Olé!

The fans loved it, but the skills weren't just for show. Manuel was stopping opposition attacks and starting new ones for Bayern. And he was still making the amazing saves that he had always made. Pep was delighted with his Number One.

'Neuer is one of the best goalkeepers in history,' the manager told the media.

That was high praise indeed. One thing that made Manuel so special was his hunger. He was a born winner and, even after the Treble, he still wanted more.

Bayern didn't lose a single Bundesliga match in that 2013–14 season until April. By then, they had already won the league. Manuel didn't get quite as many clean sheets, but his teammates scored a lot more goals. 7-0, 6-1, 4-0, 5-1 – when they played at their best, they were unbelievable.

'Now we just need to play like that in the Champions League too,' Manuel said to Dante.

They were through to the Champions League
semi-finals, but they hadn't played very well against
Arsenal or Manchester United. Real Madrid would
be much tougher opponents. One tiny mistake and
Ronaldo and Benzema would score for sure.

That's exactly what happened at the Bernabeu.
Real scored an early goal and, despite having lots
of possession, Bayern couldn't equalise. It was a
disappointing result, but there was still the second
leg at the Allianz Arena.

'Real have never won here in Munich,' Pep told
his players before kick-off. 'This isn't over yet!'

The manager's message was clear – attack and
score. With the defence pushing forward, it was a
good thing that Manuel was the best sweeper keeper
around. He was alert to every sign of danger. He
rushed off his goal line to block crosses and to clear
through-balls. But he couldn't stop Sergio Ramos's
flying header.

'Who was marking him?' Manuel complained.

A few minutes later, Ramos scored another header.
2-0.

'Offside!' Manuel screamed, raising his arm.

He looked at the linesman, but the linesman kept his flag down. Bayern were in big trouble. All Manuel could do was keep going.

'Come on, we can't concede another goal,' he shouted to Dante and Jérôme.

But they did. On the counter-attack, Gareth Bale passed to Ronaldo in the penalty area. He had all the space and time in the world to pick his spot – through the goalkeeper's legs. Nutmeg!

'Why aren't you defending?' Manuel shouted, punching the air in frustration. 'You can't just give up like that!'

It was embarrassing, humiliating. Bayern lost 4-0 in their own stadium, in front of their own fans. Top teams didn't lose big games like that.

But at the final whistle, Manuel didn't storm off and blame the tactics or his teammates. They had to stick together and come back stronger from the setback.

'We're still learning,' Manuel said with one arm around Franck and the other around Toni. Even after such a painful defeat, they walked around the Allianz Arena, clapping the fans. 'We got it wrong tonight but that won't happen again.'

The season was far from a disaster, though. Bayern had won the League and Cup Double and Manuel still had one more chance to make it a Treble – the 2014 World Cup.

CHAPTER 21

WORLD CUP 2014

'I've never seen a better sweeper,' Germany's old keeper Andreas Köpke said, 'apart from maybe Franz Beckenbauer.'

Köpke was, of course, talking about Manuel. Everyone was talking about Manuel, after his Man of the Match performance against Algeria in the 2014 World Cup's Round of 16.

All of Manuel's work with Pep at Bayern was helping Germany too. They didn't have the quickest defence at the World Cup, but that didn't matter with Manuel sweeping behind them. Everything felt so much safer with him there.

Per Mertesacker couldn't keep up with Algeria's

striker Islam Slimani, but Manuel could. As he
rushed out of his goal, he didn't dive in recklessly. He
didn't want to let his team down by getting sent off.
Instead, Manuel played like a defender. He waited
and then timed his tackle perfectly.

'Thanks, Manu!' Per shouted.

Manuel rescued his defenders again and again. He
was always ready to come out of his penalty area and
clear the danger with his feet or his head.

At first, the Germany fans held their breath
whenever Manuel sprinted out of his goal. 'What if
he makes a mistake?' they thought. But there was
no need to worry. Their brave and bold Number One
knew exactly what he was doing.

'Maybe we can catch him off his line!' the Algeria
players thought. They were desperately trying to find
a way to get past Manuel.

In extra time, they tried to lob the ball over his
head, but he was prepared for that too. *Saved!* When
it was necessary, Manuel was happy to use his hands
in the box.

With their sweeper keeper working wonders at

the back, Germany finally scored the goals to win the match.

'Manu, you really saved us today,' Toni said at the end, looking very relieved.

'Happy to help,' he replied with a smile.

Manuel had been helping his teammates all tournament. Even in the 4-0 group win over Portugal, he made a super save to keep out one of Ronaldo's powerful free kicks. As the matches got more and more difficult, Germany relied on Manuel more and more.

'Don't worry, I'm here!' he called out to his centre-backs, Jérôme and Mats Hummels.

At the amazing Maracanã Stadium in Rio de Janeiro, Germany were playing France in the World Cup quarter-final. Manuel knew it was going to be a tough battle. He was up against Real Madrid striker Karim Benzema again, plus young stars Antoine Griezmann and Paul Pogba. But Manuel believed in his team. With so much spirit and hunger to win, they could beat anyone.

Once Mats scored an early goal, it was time for

Germany to defend. It was time for Manuel to shine.

He reacted quickly to dive down and stop Mathieu Valbuena's shot. *Saved!*

He jumped up to catch Raphaël Varane's header. *Saved!*

He punched away Blaise Matuidi's strike. *Saved!*

He batted away Benzema's shot with his strong right arm. *Saved!*

At last, the referee blew the final whistle – Germany 1 France 0. Manuel threw his arms up in the air and ran to celebrate with his teammates.

'We're into the semis!' he cheered, bouncing up and down with Bastian.

Germany were one game away from another World Cup Final. But the team standing in their way were Brazil, the tournament hosts and five-time winners. They were desperate to win again in front of their home fans.

'It's going to be the eleven of us against over 200 million people!' Mesut joked.

The crowd was a sea of yellow at the Estádio Mineirão in Belo Horizonte. Even without Neymar and Thiago Silva, Brazil were still the favourites. But Germany were about to spoil their party.

Manuel couldn't believe what he was seeing. Thomas got the first goal, then Miroslav, then two from Toni and one from Sami. With thirty minutes gone, they were beating Brazil 5-0! Surely, the match was already over? But Manuel wanted to make 100 per cent sure.

'Focus!' he told his defenders. 'There's still an hour to go.'

Manuel had a busy start to the second half. He blocked Ramires' cross and then Oscar's shot. But best of all was his double save to deny Paulinho. The Brazilian looked certain to score the rebound, but Manuel got back up quickly and threw his arms in front of the ball. *Saved!*

'Thanks, Manu!' Per shouted.

After battling bravely through that storm, Germany went up the other end and grabbed two more goals. 7-0! It was too good to be true. In the very last minute, Oscar scored to take Manuel's clean sheet away. That was a disappointment, but he certainly wasn't complaining.

'We're into the final!' Manuel cheered, bouncing up and down with Bastian. It was the greatest night of his Germany career, and maybe the greatest night in German football history.

First France, then Brazil, and now Germany faced Argentina, featuring Lionel Messi and Gonzalo Higuaín, in the World Cup Final. Could they beat them again, just like they had in 2010? That time, Germany had won 4-0 but this time, it was much more difficult.

'Keep going, the goal will come!' Manuel shouted to his tired teammates.

For 112 minutes, the two nations were tied at 0-0. Argentina couldn't score past Manuel, and Germany couldn't score past Sergio Romero either.

As the minutes ticked by, Manuel began to think ahead. Would there be another penalty shoot-out? And if so, could he be Germany's hero? He had a great record with Schalke and Bayern, but this was totally different. This was the World Cup Final.

'I can do it,' Manuel kept telling himself. There was no-one better under pressure.

But in the end, there were no penalties to save. Mario Götze finally volleyed home the only goal of the game and Germany held on for the victory.

'We did it!' Manuel cheered with all of his teammates.

Their dream had finally come true. They had fallen at the semi-final stage at the 2010 World Cup and at Euro 2012, but they never gave up. Now, in 2014, Germany were the Champions of the World.

'Champions of the World' – Manuel loved the sound of those words. He chanted them again and again during that incredible night at the Maracanã, until he lost his voice.

Could life get any better? Manuel had a World Cup winner's medal around his neck, plus the Golden Glove trophy in his hands. It was official; he was the best goalkeeper in the tournament, the best goalkeeper in the world. With his saves and his sweeping, Manuel had led his country to glory.

MORE TO WIN?

'What do you give a man who has everything?'
Marcel wrote as a joke in Manuel's twenty-ninth
birthday card.

That was a good question. Manuel had already
won the German League twice and he was about
to make it a hat-trick. On top of that, there was the
German Cup, the Champions League, the FIFA Club
World Cup and the World Cup. Manuel was the
UEFA Goalkeeper of the Year, the German Footballer
of the Year, and he had even finished third in the
2014 Ballon d'Or, just behind Messi and Ronaldo.
What was there left to achieve?

'Plenty,' was Manuel's quick reply. 'I've got plenty
more to win!'

The top thing on his win-list was a second Champions League title. The Bayern team was getting better and better. They now had Xabi Alonso in midfield and his old rival Robert Lewandowski up front.

'I'm just glad that you're not shooting at me anymore!' Manuel joked with Robert. 'I always hated playing against Dortmund because of you.'

Bayern thrashed Porto to set up a semi-final against Pep's old team, Barcelona. Manuel was facing Messi again.

'Bring it on!' he cheered. You could only be the best by beating the best.

At the Nou Camp, Manuel won almost every battle. He saved shots from Luis Suárez and Dani Alves with his long legs. He caught a long-range strike from Messi, and he rushed out to tackle Neymar.

'Bayern Munich have a great goalkeeper,' the TV commentator said. 'Barcelona will have to work hard to beat him.'

But eventually, they did beat Manuel. He was the winner in the 2014 World Cup Final but this time, it was Messi's night. For his amazing second goal, he chipped the ball over Manuel's diving body. Sometimes, the Argentinian wizard was just *too* good.

'Come on, we can't defend that badly and get away with it,' Pep told his players afterwards. 'Even Manuel can't save us every time!'

But Bayern didn't learn their lesson. One year later, in spring 2016, Bayern faced Atlético Madrid in the Champions League semi-final. Saúl Ñíguez dribbled past Thiago, then Juan Bernat, then Xabi Alonso.

'Someone make a tackle!' Manuel screamed out as Ñíguez entered the penalty area. 'Please!'

But no-one did and Atlético scored.

In the second leg, Bayern pushed forward, and left the defending to Manuel. On the counter-attack, Antoine Griezmann dribbled through and scored the crucial away goal. The Allianz Arena fell silent in shock.

'We're cursed,' Jérôme muttered moodily as the Bayern players trudged off the pitch. 'We've now lost three Champions League semi-finals in a row!'

Manuel shook his head. He was a responsible senior player now, and he didn't want to hear any excuses.

'There's no such thing as curses, J. We only have ourselves to blame. We made mistakes and we got punished – it's as simple as that! It's no good feeling sorry for ourselves. We have to come back stronger. Remember when we lost in the semi-finals of the 2010 World Cup and then Euro 2012 with Germany? Those defeats were so painful, but they definitely made us a tougher team in 2014.'

But what about Euro 2016? Were Germany still the toughest team around? Could they win back-to-back international tournaments in France?

'Of course we can!' Manuel argued. It was one of the few trophies that he didn't yet have.

He had good reason to feel confident. Most of his old friends were still there with him – Mesut, Benedikt, Mats, Sami, Jérôme, Toni and Bastian. Only Philipp, Per and Miroslav had retired. Germany had a brilliant team of players who knew each other inside out.

'I want to go out with a bang!' new skipper Bastian told them.

In Germany's first four games, Manuel didn't concede a single goal. He didn't have many saves to make, but when his teammates needed him, he was always there.

Ukraine's Yevhen Konoplyanka beat Benedikt to the ball and hit a fierce shot from the edge of the penalty area... *Saved!*

Slovakia's Juraj Kucka outjumped Joshua Kimmich at the back post. His header flew towards the top corner... *Saved!*

Manuel was enjoying himself and Germany were through to the quarter-finals.

'We can't get carried away,' coach Joachim Löw warned his players. 'Every game is a big final now!'

Manuel couldn't wait to face Italy, the team that knocked them out of Euro 2012. Four years on, it was time for sweet revenge.

'Come on boys, we can't let them beat us again!' Manuel clapped and cheered.

With Bastian on the bench, he was Germany's

captain. It was a proud honour and it made Manuel even more determined to lead his country to the semi-finals and beyond.

After 120 minutes of tense football, the match went to penalties. Manuel prepared himself for his big moment. It was his job to save the day for Germany.

'Manu, we believe in you!' Bastian shouted, giving him a hug.

Manuel bounced up and down on his goal line. It was one-on-one, his favourite battle. He stared into the eyes of each opponent:

Manuel dived one way, and Lorenzo Insigne went the other… *Goal!*

Simone Zaza went for lots of power… *Miss!*

Manuel dived to his left, but Andrea Barzagli went down the middle… *Goal!*

Graziano Pellè dragged his shot to the left… *Miss!*

It was 2-2 as Leonardo Bonucci stepped up for Italy. He had already scored a penalty against Manuel during the match.

'You're not scoring another!' Germany's goalkeeper thought to himself.

This time, Manuel guessed the right way… *Saved!*

He didn't celebrate at all. It wasn't over yet. He just pulled up his socks and waited.

Bastian had the chance to win it for Germany. He aimed high into the top corner… *Miss!*

The shoot-out went to sudden death. Italy scored, then Germany scored, Italy scored, then Germany scored, Italy scored, then Germany scored. When would it ever end? Manuel needed to save one before one of his teammates missed one.

Italy's Matteo Darmian struck his penalty low… *Saved!*

Again, Manuel didn't celebrate, not until Jonas Hector scored the winner for Germany. Then he sprinted towards his teammates.

'You did it, Manu!' Bastian cheered. 'You're a hero!'

Unfortunately, after all that excitement in the quarter-final, Germany lost another semi-final. France just had too much energy for them, especially with the home crowd behind them. Griezmann scored twice, and Manuel's Euro 2016 was over. He was starting to really hate semi-finals.

CHAPTER 22

CAPTAIN MANUEL

After Euro 2016, Bastian retired from international football. So, who would be the next captain of Germany? There was really only one man for the job. The man who had captained his country through most of that tournament anyway: Manuel.

'He has everything that I want from a captain,' coach Joachim Löw explained to the media. 'As well as being a great player, he is a team player, a leader and a role model.'

At first, Manuel was too proud for words. Captain of Germany! It was beyond his wildest dreams as a young boy in Gelsenkirchen. But eventually, he had to speak.

'It's a huge honour for me, of course, but we need

lots of leaders on the pitch if we're going to succeed,' he said modestly.

To really 'succeed', Germany would need to win the 2018 World Cup in Russia. No country had won back-to-back trophies since Pelé's Brazil. Manuel put that goal to the back of his mind.

'First, we need to qualify!' he told his teammates.

Manuel could handle high pressure. That's what made him such a good goalkeeper, and such a good captain too. He kept three clean sheets as Germany beat Norway, the Czech Republic and Northern Ireland.

'Right, I want ten wins out of ten!' Manuel decided.

Amazingly, Germany did achieve that target, but they had to do most of it without their new captain.

Bayern's Champions League quarter-final against Real Madrid in April 2017 went from bad to worse. First, Arturo was wrongly sent off, and then Ronaldo scored a goal that was clearly offside.

'How could you not see that?' Manuel screamed at the linesman. 'He was miles off!'

That wasn't the end of it, though. As Manuel

rushed out of his goal to close down Marcelo, his left foot slipped on the grass. He felt a fierce, sharp pain.

'Arghhhhhhhhh!' he screamed, collapsing to the floor.

Ronaldo scored but Manuel had bigger problems than that. Even though he could barely walk, he had to carry on. Bayern had used up all their substitutions.

'Just stand in goal!' his teammates told him, but that wasn't Manuel's style. He was an all-action keeper.

As soon as the match was over, he was rushed off for medical tests. The news wasn't good.

'I'm afraid there's a fracture,' the doctor said, showing Manuel the X-ray.

'Is it serious?' he asked. He didn't know much about injuries because he hadn't had many. Until now.

The doctor nodded, 'You'll be out for at least eight weeks, Manu. It's April now, so focus on getting yourself fit for next season.'

Next season? That felt *so* far away! What was Manuel going to do without football? He didn't like missing one match, so missing months of matches was going to be very, very difficult.

'Please don't rush your recovery,' new Bayern manager Carlo Ancelotti told him. 'Bones take time to heal, okay?'

'Okay,' he agreed reluctantly.

Manuel counted down the days until he could get back in the gym, and then back to full fitness. He didn't realise just how much he loved football until it was taken away. He listened to music, he ate delicious food, he worked on his children's charity, but nothing else gave him quite the same buzz.

'I *need* to play football!' he moaned at the TV.

The closest Manuel got was going out on the pitch in May 2017 to celebrate Bayern's fourth consecutive Bundesliga title. He had played twenty-six league games before his injury.

'I do get a winner's medal, right?' he asked, looking anxious.

'Of course!'

As the fans cheered his name, Manuel felt more determined than ever to return to what he did best – playing football.

'I'll be back soon!' he promised his teammates.

They needed him. When Philipp retired in July 2017, Manuel became the new captain of Bayern Munich. He was now the leader of club and country.

'Wow, that's a lot of responsibility,' his proud parents said. 'It's a good thing you've got those broad shoulders!'

Manuel missed the German Super Cup victory over Dortmund, but he made his big comeback in the second week of the 2017–18 Bundesliga season. It turned out to be a perfect Bayern return – another win, and another clean sheet.

'Welcome back, we missed you!' Mats said, giving him a big hug.

'I missed you too,' Manuel replied happily. 'It's great to be back!'

The good times didn't last, however. After only four games, Manuel broke the same bone in his left foot again.

'Nooooooo!' he cried out on the training pitch. He knew straight away that it was the same injury.

It was a disaster. This time, Manuel needed a bigger operation, which meant missing even more football.

'We hope Manuel will be back in January 2018,' chairman Karl-Heinz Rummenigge announced.

Many Bayern Munich and Germany fans were worried about their goalkeeper's future. What if the injury kept happening again and again?

But worrying wasn't Manuel's style. He had to stay strong and think positively.

'When it comes to the 2018 World Cup, nothing will stand in my way!' he told the media.

Manuel had suffered many setbacks during his football career, from doubts over his height when he was younger all the way through to disappointing semi-final defeats. But every time, he bounced back stronger and kept on winning.

That was one of the many things that made Manuel the best goalkeeper in the world. Germany's sweeper keeper could do it all – saves, kicks, throws, tackles, passes. He had the talent and he had the *nervenstärke* too – the mental strength to handle the pressure. Five Bundesliga titles, one Champions League trophy and one World Cup just wasn't enough for him. Manuel always wanted more.

Turn the page for a special bonus
chapter of Manuel Neuer's journey to
the World Cup . . .

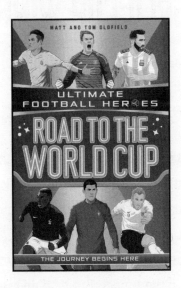

Chapter taken from *Road to the World Cup*
by Matt and Tom Oldfield

Available now!

PART ONE

WORLD CUP WINNER

Maracanã Stadium, 13 July 2014

As Manuel sang the words of the German national anthem loud and proud, he tried not to look over at the famous gold trophy sitting a few metres away from him. It was so beautiful and so close. Manuel could have reached out and touched it when he walked out of the tunnel. But he didn't want to jinx it. The trophy didn't belong to them. Yet.

'Come on!' Manuel clapped as the music finished.

The famous Maracanã stadium in Rio de Janeiro was packed and ready for the 2014 World Cup Final – Germany vs Argentina. Manuel had lost in the semi-finals of the 2010 World Cup and Euro 2012 but this time, Germany had made it all the way to the final. After thrashing the hosts Brazil 7–1, they were the favourites to win, but they couldn't underestimate a top team like Argentina.

'We can do this!' Manuel told the defenders.

Philipp Lahm, Mats Hummels, Jérôme Boateng and Benedikt Höwedes – they were more than just his teammates for club and country. They were his friends. They believed in each other and worked together. That's why they were one game away from becoming Champions of the World.

Yes, Argentina had Lionel Messi, but Germany had Manuel. In Brazil, he had shown that he was the best goalkeeper in the world. It wasn't just his incredible reaction saves; it was his all-round game.

After his match-winning performance against Algeria, Germany's old keeper Andreas Köpke had given him the ultimate praise – 'I've never seen a better sweeper, apart from maybe Franz Beckenbauer.'

No, Manuel was no ordinary keeper. He could catch, stop, tackle *and* pass. He was Germany's last line of defence and also their first line of attack. His teammates trusted him and relied on him.

'Jérôme, watch Messi when he drops deep!'
Manuel called and pointed.

He never stopped moving, talking, organising. It
all helped him to keep his concentration for the big
moments, the moments when Germany would need
their goalkeeper to save the day.

After thirty minutes, Gonzalo Higuaín had the ball
in the net. As he dived down, Manuel already had
his arm up. 'Offside!' he called out.

Manuel was right, of course. The linesman raised
his flag. No goal – what a relief!

In the second half, Higuaín chased after a long
ball. He used his speed to escape from the German
defenders, but he couldn't escape from the German
goalkeeper. Manuel to the rescue! He sprinted off his
line to jump and punch the ball away from danger.

'Thanks, Manu!' Benedikt shouted, patting him on
the back.

Manuel nodded modestly. He was just doing his
job: number one sweeper keeper.

Argentina couldn't score past Manuel, but Germany
couldn't score past Sergio Romero either. The longer

the match went on, the more nerve-wracking it
became, for the fans and for the players. Fortunately,
Manuel was Mr Nervenstärke – he had nerves of
steel. Even though he was the last man, he stayed
calm and focused.

In the last ten minutes, Germany had several
chances to score.

'So close!' Manuel groaned, putting his hands on
his head.

But he didn't switch off. He had to concentrate at
all times. A goalkeeper never knew when his team
would need him. In extra-time, Rodrigo Palacio
chested the ball down and ran into the penalty area.
Manuel was out in a flash, making it hard for the
striker to score. Palacio managed to chip the ball over
him, but it went wide of the goal.

'No more mistakes!' Manuel ordered.

He was already preparing himself for his favourite
battle – penalties. One on one, goalkeeper vs striker,
the pressure, the drama – Manuel loved it all. He
had been the shoot-out hero so many times before,
for Schalke and for Bayern Munich, but never for

Germany. Would this be his moment?

No, because André Schürrle crossed to Mario Götze, who volleyed the ball into the net. What a goal – Germany 1 Argentina 0!

Most of the players and fans went wild, but not Manuel. He punched the air and then returned to his goal line. There were still six minutes of football left to play before he could celebrate properly.

'Stay organised!' he screamed out.

Lucas Biglia flicked the ball into the path of Marcos Rojo. Danger! Manuel had one last bit of sweeper keeping to do. He rushed out, lifted the ball over Rojo's head and caught it on the other side. He made it look so easy.

Neuer! Neuer! Neuer!

It was the perfect way for Manuel to end a perfect tournament. At the final whistle, he ran and jumped onto the growing pile of his Germany teammates. He hugged every single one of them.

'We did it!' they cheered.

Back in 2009, Manuel had won the Under-21 European Championships with Mats, Jérôme,

Benedikt, Sami Khedira and Mesut Özil. That night, they dreamt about the future. Now, that future had arrived. They had won the World Cup together.

Manuel put on a white Germany shirt over his green goalkeeper jersey. He wanted to wear the national colours and he was no different to the outfield players anyway. But soon he had to take it off because he had a special award to collect.

'...And the Golden Glove for Best Goalkeeper goes to... MANUEL NEUER!'

Manuel had kept out Cristiano Ronaldo's Portugal, Karim Benzema's France, Hulk's Brazil and finally Messi's Argentina. He was the number one sweeper keeper, the best in the world.

Manuel raised the trophy in one big hand and punched the air with the other. What a night! He was very proud of his own achievement, but he was even prouder of his team's achievement. The World Cup was the trophy that Manuel really wanted to hold. It was his childhood dream come true.

'Yessssssssssssssssssss!' he shouted, lifting it high above his head.

MANUEL NEUER
HONOURS

Schalke

🏆 DFB-Pokal (German Cup): 2010 –11

Bayern Munich

🏆 Bundesliga: 2012–13, 2013–14, 2014–15, 2015–16, 2016–17

🏆 DFB-Pokal: 2012–13, 2013–14, 2015–16

🏆 DFL-Supercup: 2012, 2016

🏆 UEFA Champions League: 2012–13

🏆 UEFA Super Cup: 2013

🏆 FIFA Club World Cup: 2013

Germany

🏆 FIFA World Cup: 2014

🏆 UEFA European Under-21 Football
Championship: 2009

Individual

🏆 Footballer of the Year in Germany: 2011, 2014

🏆 UEFA Goalkeeper of the Year: 2011, 2013, 2014,
2015

🏆 UEFA Euro Team of the Tournament: 2012

🏆 2013 UEFA Champions League Final: Fans' Man
of the Match

🏆 IFFHS World's Best Goalkeeper: 2013, 2014,
2015, 2016

🏆 FIFA FIFPro World XI: 2013, 2014, 2015, 2016

🏆 UEFA Team of the Year: 2013, 2014, 2015

🏆 FIFA World Cup Golden Glove: 2014

🏆 FIFA World Cup All-Star Team: 2014

🏆 Bundesliga Team of the Year: 2014–15, 2015–
16, 2016–17

NEUER

1 THE FACTS

NAME: MANUEL PETER NEUER

DATE OF BIRTH: 27 March 1986

AGE: 32

PLACE OF BIRTH: Gelsenkirchen

NATIONALITY: Germany

BEST FRIEND: Bastian Schweinsteiger

CURRENT CLUB: Bayern Munich

POSITION: GK

THE STATS

Height (cm):	**193**
Club appearances:	**531**
Club goals:	**0**
Club trophies:	**14**
International appearances:	**74**
International goals:	**0**
International trophies:	**2**
Ballon d'Ors:	**0**

★ ★ ★ **HERO RATING: 90** ★ ★ ★

GREATEST MOMENTS

Type and search the web links to see the magic for yourself!

18 JULY 2005, SERBIA AND MONTENEGRO 4-2 GERMANY

https://www.youtube.com/watch?v=msyHnlnooyY

The Germany Under-19s got off to a terrible start at the European Championships in Northern Ireland, despite Manuel's brilliant goalkeeping. With the score at 2-2, he made a brilliant diving stop to keep out Borko Veselinović's spot-kick. That was the first of many amazing penalty saves. With the pressure on, Manuel loved to be the hero.

5 MARCH 2008, PORTO 1-0 SCHALKE (SCHALKE WON 4-1 ON PENALTIES)

https://www.youtube.com/watch?v=HY-0xuJ0edM

In his very first season in the Champions League, Manuel showed that he belonged at the top level. In the second leg against Porto, he made save after save after save to keep Schalke in the game. When the tie went to penalties, there was only going to be one hero. Manuel saved two spot-kicks to win the shoot-out!

26 APRIL 2011, SCHALKE 0-2 MANCHESTER UNITED

https://www.youtube.com/watch?v=dcNZiDWPBck

Three years later, Manuel put on another masterclass in the Champions League semi-final against Manchester United. Schalke lost 2-0 but without their amazing Number One, it could have been 7, 8, maybe even 10-0! Sir Alex Ferguson said that it was the best goalkeeping performance he had ever seen against his team.

25 MAY 2013, BORUSSIA DORTMUND 1-2 BAYERN MUNICH

https://www.youtube.com/watch?v=wA4ChhQ38GQ

After the disappointment of losing in the 2012 Champions League Final, Bayern bounced back brilliantly to win it the next year. Manuel had to be at his very best to keep out Robert Lewandowski and co. at Wembley. After the victory, he was named the fans' Man of the Match. A week later, Manuel helped Bayern to make it a historic Treble.

30 JUNE 2014, GERMANY 2-1 ALGERIA

https://www.youtube.com/watch?v=TOL3A9Y_eOM

When Germany needed their goalkeeper to save the day, Manuel didn't let them down. In the second round of the 2014 World Cup, he showed off his full range of sweeper keeper skills – punching, throwing, tackling, even heading! Thanks to Manuel, Germany made it through to the quarter-finals, and the rest is history.

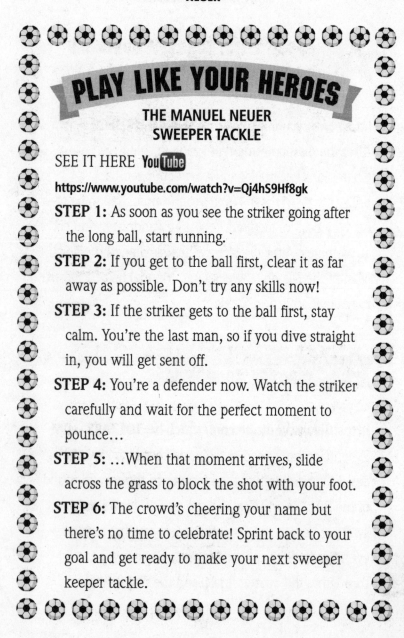

PLAY LIKE YOUR HEROES

THE MANUEL NEUER SWEEPER TACKLE

SEE IT HERE YouTube

https://www.youtube.com/watch?v=Qj4hS9Hf8gk

STEP 1: As soon as you see the striker going after the long ball, start running.

STEP 2: If you get to the ball first, clear it as far away as possible. Don't try any skills now!

STEP 3: If the striker gets to the ball first, stay calm. You're the last man, so if you dive straight in, you will get sent off.

STEP 4: You're a defender now. Watch the striker carefully and wait for the perfect moment to pounce...

STEP 5: ...When that moment arrives, slide across the grass to block the shot with your foot.

STEP 6: The crowd's cheering your name but there's no time to celebrate! Sprint back to your goal and get ready to make your next sweeper keeper tackle.

TEST YOUR KNOWLEDGE

QUESTIONS

1. How old was Manuel when he got his first football?

2. What position did Manuel play at first?

3. Who were Manuel's three main goalkeeper heroes?

4. Which two other future Germany internationals went to Gesamtschule Berger Feld School with Manuel?

5. How tall did the doctor predict that Manuel would become?

6. Manuel kept a clean sheet in his Bundesliga debut for Schalke – true or false?

7. When did Manuel become Germany's Number One?

8. Which other top European club wanted to buy Manuel, before he moved to Bayern Munich?

9. Who scored the winning penalty past Manuel in the 2012 Champions League Final?

10. Manuel won the 2014 Ballon d'Or – true or false?

11. Who did Manuel replace as the captain of a) Germany and b) Bayern Munich?

Answers below. . . No cheating!

1. Two years old 2. Striker 3. Oliver Kahn, Edwin van der Sar and Jens Lehmann 4. Benedikt Höwedes and Mesut Özil 5. Six feet two 6. True – Schalke beat Aachen 1-0 7. At the 2010 World Cup 8. Manchester United 9. Chelsea's Didier Drogba 11. False – He finished third, behind Cristiano Ronaldo and Lionel Messi. 11. a) Bastian Schweinsteiger and b) Philipp Lahm

This summer, your favourite football heroes will pull on their country's colours to go head-to-head for the ultimate prize – the World Cup.

Celebrate by making sure you have six of the best Ultimate Football Heroes, now with limited-edition international covers!

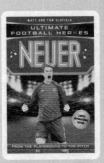

FOLLOW IN THE FOOTSTEPS OF LEGENDS. . .

Bridge the gap between past and present by stepping into the shoes of six classic World Cup heroes and reading their exciting stories – from the playground to the pitch, and to superstardom!

COMING 31ST MAY

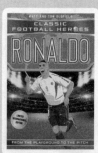